Politics

T0056319

Why It Matters

In these short and lively books, world-leading thinkers make the case for the importance of their subjects and aim to inspire a new generation of students.

Helen Beebee & Michael Rush, *Philosophy*
Robert Eaglestone, *Literature*
Andrew Gamble, *Politics*
Lynn Hunt, *History*
Tim Ingold, *Anthropology*
Neville Morley, *Classics*
Alexander B. Murphy, *Geography*
Geoffrey K. Pullum, *Linguistics*
Graham Ward, *Theology and Religion*

Andrew Gamble

———————

Politics

Why It Matters

polity

Copyright © Andrew Gamble 2019

The right of Andrew Gamble to be identified as Author of this Work has been asserted in accordance with the UK Copyright, Designs and Patents Act 1988.

First published in 2019 by Polity Press

Polity Press
65 Bridge Street
Cambridge CB2 1UR, UK

Polity Press
101 Station Landing
Suite 300
Medford, MA 02155, USA

ISBN-13: 978-1-5095-2728-1
ISBN-13: 978-1-5095-2729-8 (pb)

A catalogue record for this book is available from the British Library.

Library of Congress Cataloging-in-Publication Data

Names: Gamble, Andrew, author.
Title: Politics : why it matters / Andrew Gamble.
Description: Cambridge ; Medford, MA : Polity Press, 2019. | Includes
  bibliographical references and index.
Identifiers: LCCN 2018033530 (print) | LCCN 2018049573 (ebook) | ISBN
  9781509527328 (Epub) | ISBN 9781509527281 (hardback) | ISBN
  9781509527298 (pbk.)
Subjects: LCSH: Political science--Philosophy.
Classification: LCC JA71 (ebook) | LCC JA71 .G252 2019 (print) | DDC 320--
dc23 LC record available at https://lccn.loc.gov/2018033530

Typeset in 11 on 15 Sabon by Servis Filmsetting Ltd, Stockport, Cheshire
Printed and bound in Great Britain by CPI Group (UK) Ltd, Croydon

For further information on Polity, visit our website: politybooks.com

For Michael Moran, 1946–2018
Scholar and friend

Someone who understood why politics matters

Contents

Preface

This book is a product of many years of thinking about politics, studying politics, teaching politics, and experiencing politics. Every generation is shaped by its political experiences and its political memories. One of my earliest political memories was in 1956 when Britain and France invaded Egypt to take back control of the Suez Canal. I had little understanding of what was happening, but it stuck in my memory principally because my father was angry enough to cancel his subscription to the *Observer*, so strongly did he disagree with their criticisms of the Government's actions. Politics obviously mattered. My formative experiences continued with the Sharpeville massacre in 1960, the Cuban missile crisis in 1962, the Profumo scandal and Kennedy's assassination in 1963, and Labour's election victory in 1964, promising a New Britain, with the improbable slogan, 'Let's go with Labour and we'll get things done.' At university between 1965 and 1968 I was swept up in the excitement of the political and cultural earthquakes of those years. One of the slogans which appeared on the walls in Paris in May 1968 captured our mood: 'Be realistic. Demand the impossible.' These experiences gave me my first involvement with politics and why it mattered. I began to study it in earnest and soon found there was a vast and fascinating hinterland of ideas and histories and arguments to explore, and that politics was a lot more complex than I had ever imagined. In writing this book, I have drawn in particular on two of my earlier publications: *Politics and Fate* (Cambridge: Polity, 2000) and *The Limits of Politics* (Cambridge: Cambridge University Press, 2009), which was my inaugural lecture at Cambridge.

I would like to thank my editors at Polity, Louise Knight and Nekane Tanaka Galdos, first for suggesting this project to me and then for giving such excellent support through the process of writing and submission, and also Justin Dyer for very thorough and helpful copy-editing, which has greatly improved the flow of the argument. I would also like to thank two anonymous reviewers and especially Adam Roble for their very helpful comments on an earlier draft. This book is dedicated to Mick Moran, whose sudden death in April 2018 robbed us of one of the best political scientists of his generation, someone who understood better than any of us why politics mattered and wrote many fine books explaining why it did. Consider this passage, read out at his funeral, which comes from his classic text *Politics and Governance in the UK*:

> Why study politics? Indeed why be concerned with political life at all? For most citizens . . . the answers to these questions are pretty obvious: there are no good reasons either to study politics or to take an active part in political life. . . . But if politics is a minority interest, even in a democracy, it is nevertheless a matter of the utmost importance – in a quite literal sense, a matter of life and death. . . . Politics is about trying to choose between competing views and interests . . . the failure to make these choices by peaceful means, and to carry them out effectively and peacefully has catastrophic results. Consider, for instance, the life of people unfortunate enough to live in poverty-stricken countries of Africa, like the Democratic Republic of Congo. What single thing would transform their life: a great medical advance, a great advance in biotechnology which would make farming more productive? Neither of these things; their lives would be transformed for the better by peace and the creation of a stable system of

government, because since the then Belgian Congo achieved independence nearly sixty years ago it has been racked by civil wars. Understanding politics, if we want to make the world a better place for our fellow human beings, is more urgent even than understanding medicine, biology or physics. Politics shapes every detail of our lives, from the most dramatic to the most mundane.[1]

This book is also for my six grandchildren, Joni, Nye, Louis, George, Ceinwen, and Ivy, who are at present blissfully unaware of politics and why it matters but one day will understand.

Andrew Gamble
Sheffield
August 2018

[1] Michael Moran, *Politics and Governance in the UK* (London, Palgrave-Macmillan, 2011), p. 6.

Introduction

Politics today has a poor reputation. This has not always been so. There have been times and cultures when it was considered one of the most noble, most elevating, and most necessary human activities. Aristotle thought that participating in the life of the *polis*, being an active citizen, speaking and acting in the public arena, were the highest goods to which human beings could aspire. It was how they showed what they were capable of. Cicero agreed. For him the highest human virtue lay in the possession and employment of knowledge in practical affairs.

The Greek *polis* (from which our word 'politics' derives) and the Roman republic (*respublica* means literally public affairs) were ideals which have been revived at various times in western politics, notably by the Founding Fathers of the United States in their vision of a virtuous republic and also by the leaders

1

of the French Revolution with their famous slogan 'Liberty, Equality, Fraternity'. Different versions of it appear in other cultural traditions, such as the Mandarin scholar-bureaucrats of China. The positive case for politics recognizes that ruling requires great skill and wisdom and that good government makes possible all the other things which human beings value. Creating and sustaining a civil and political order which maintains civility by keeping conflict between its citizens within limits and guarantees certain liberties is a remarkable achievement whenever and wherever it occurs. We often fail to appreciate what a prize it is.

Some of this still lingers in ideals of public service and public virtue, but it has had to contend with another tradition which focuses not on the prize, a civil and political order which keeps the peace, but on the process of politics. Allowing a degree of conflict between citizens makes politics noisy and messy. It is easy to see no more in politics than the self-interested pursuit of power, which makes politics as an activity seem disreputable, oppressive, and corrupt, something to be avoided and if possible suppressed. From this perspective, politics is regarded as consisting of knavery, double-dealing, and trickery, and little else. The British national anthem, 'God Save the King', written and composed

2

in the eighteenth century, has a revealing second verse which is not sung very often nowadays. It confidently denounces the seditious Scots: 'Confound their politics, frustrate their knavish tricks.' Politics and knavish tricks go together in most people's minds.

In the Republican party primaries in the United States in 2016, the ferocity with which candidates ostensibly from the same party sought to abuse and destroy one another confirmed a widely held view of politics. The pursuit of power and the unscrupulous means politicians will often embrace to win has always been part of the allure of politics to those who participate in the great game and helps explain the mixture of fascination and distaste towards politics in those who do not.

The distaste is real but so too is the fascination. Politics is an endless drama of character and circumstance, and this is what drives news agendas all over the world. People regularly say they are bored with politics and not interested in it, yet the news media are filled with little else. How do we explain this? In part it is because there are different kinds of politics.

The kind of politics most of the news media are concerned with has much less interest in the details and complexities of public policy than in the personalities, the scandals, the power struggles, the fiascos, the rise and fall of particular individuals. They concentrate on the trivia of politics, which they weave into compelling narratives and morality tales which focus disproportionately on the negative side of politics, leaving many citizens feeling that no-one can be trusted, no-one is competent, no-one is honest or public-spirited. Everyone is out for what they can get. As Groucho Marx put it in his satirical take on politicians: 'These are my principles, and if you don't like them ... well, I have others.' Contemporary satirists have not been slow to spot the frequent absurdity of modern politics arising from the frenzy and paranoia which often surrounds it. One of the most popular UK television series of recent years, *The Thick of It*, portrays the modern political world as dominated by short-term crises brought about by the competitive pressure to secure favourable headlines to the exclusion of almost everything else.

If this was all there was to politics, there would not be much to understand and few would take the trouble to do so, still less to devote their lives to studying it and writing about it. Most people, even as they disparage politics and politicians, have a deeper intuition that there is more to politics than the occasionally bizarre and self-seeking behaviour of some politicians. This is one reason why politics deserves our attention. Politics is everywhere. It underpins the lives we lead. With all its shortcomings, it is only through politics, and different kinds of politics, that some of the pressing problems we face can be addressed.

This book is aimed at showing why that is so, and why the study of politics can be so enthralling and absorbing, as well as so important to how we live and to the future prospects of the varied societies and cultures human beings have created. To study politics you need to have hope in the potential of human beings and human societies and what they have accomplished and are capable of accomplishing, but also a sceptical awareness of the limits of human knowledge and human capacities, the frailty of human societies and of individual human beings, both their darker and their absurd sides. As Napoleon once remarked, and he had some experience in the matter, 'From the sublime to the ridiculous is only one step.' Some politicians never rise above the ridiculous, and for those who reach the sublime the experience is fleeting. For the Japanese Samurai it lasted no longer than the cherry blossom in springtime. Shelley's poem on Ozymandias notes the transience of the power of even the most dominant and despotic rulers.

Introduction

I met a traveller from an antique land,
Who said: 'Two vast and trunkless legs of stone
Stand in the desert. . . . Near them, on the sand,
Half sunk a shattered visage lies, . . .
And on the pedestal, these words appear:
My name is Ozymandias, King of Kings;
Look on my Works, ye Mighty, and despair!
Nothing beside remains. Round the decay
Of that colossal Wreck, boundless and bare
The lone and level sands stretch far away.'

There are many contemporary despotic authoritarian rulers like Ozymandias. Some of them come to violent ends; others die peacefully in their beds. In the rough exchanges of democratic politics, democratic politicians are often compared to despots and authoritarian rulers. But we should always remember the difference.

1

Why Bother with Politics?

The case against politics can seem compelling. Has not politics been responsible for the wars, civil wars, rebellions, and revolutions which have regularly devastated societies, liquidating and impoverishing vast numbers, and destroying the things which make human lives worth living? During the civil war in seventeenth-century England, which also engulfed Scotland, Ireland, and Wales, Thomas Hobbes wrote *Leviathan*, which vividly depicted the consequences of political breakdown, and the return of human beings to a state of nature:

> During the time men live without a common power to keep them all in awe, they are in that condition called war; and such a war, as is of every man, against every man. . . . In such condition, there is no place for industry . . . no arts; no letters; no society;

> and which is worst of all, continual fear, and danger
> of violent death; and the life of man, solitary, poor,
> nasty, brutish, and short.[1]

Hobbes argued that war is the default condition of human existence. The utmost skill is needed to design and manage a state that keeps its political conflicts within strict limits and prevents social order from breaking down. He thought a kind of despotism – meaning the absolute rule of one person or group of persons – able to suppress conflict and therefore to suppress politics was a price worth paying for civil peace. One objection to Hobbes is that politics may be suppressed for the citizens but it still goes on in the court around the ruler. The political world in an authoritarian state is narrower than in a republic or a democracy but it is still there. So even in times of peace, even when a power has arisen to provide order, the political world goes on as it always has, dominated by force and fraud, greed and corruption. Nowhere is this more evident than in the absolute monarchies, theocracies, and dictatorships which have formed the great majority of the political systems under which human beings have lived for the past five thousand years. Despotic

[1] Thomas Hobbes, *Leviathan* (Oxford: Basil Blackwell, 1946), ch. 13, p. 82.

rule has been the norm in states, in civil associations, and in households for most of recorded human history. There have been enlightened despots, just despots, humane despots, reforming despots in all cultures, but they remained despots, and were often succeeded by rulers who were not enlightened, just, humane, or reforming. Under authoritarian rule the checks against arbitrary power, greed, and corruption are always weak.

Surely democracies are different? The great hope of the modern era has been that the closed world of autocracy and authoritarianism can be replaced by the open world of representative government, respecting minorities and human rights, guaranteeing free speech and free association, and making rulers accountable. The rights that democracies enshrine have been bitterly fought for, and when new democracies have been formed, as with the ending of the apartheid regime in South Africa in 1994, there have often been outpourings of hope and enthusiasm and a belief that anything is possible. But the euphoria rarely lasts; indeed in the case of South Africa it scarcely outlived the end of Nelson Mandela's presidency. Politics in democracies, new and old, although almost always better than the oppressive authoritarian rule it replaces, still often disappoints. To many citizens, democratic politics, if not oppressive, remains grubby, disreputable, boring, remote, alienating, and never seems to change much, or when it does only gradually and in small, incremental ways.

Occasionally in democracies there are moments when the sovereign people is called upon to make a decision that is critical for the future of the country. The 2016 Brexit referendum in the UK was widely regarded as such a moment. The country was deeply divided, and the majority to leave the European Union was narrow – 52 per cent to 48 per cent. Among the supporters of Leave – many of whom had not believed they would be victorious right up until the voting trend became clear on the night – there was euphoria. Many genuinely thought this was a decisive movement of national renewal, a new beginning. The supporters of Remain were distraught, because the result struck at an important part of their identity, their sense of being European as well as British citizens and part of a European community.

The aftermath of the vote has been underwhelming for both sides. The long and complex negotiations to extricate Britain from the EU and maintain some kind of consensus within the nation, within Parliament, and within the political parties has turned Brexit into a swamp of vagueness and indecision into which the whole nation has gradually been sinking deeper and deeper. Instead of a clean break, it seems an unending process which has sucked energy from everything else, and may end up leaving Britain's relationship to the EU little changed, except in symbolic terms (blue passports instead of red ones). The country, however, may be substantially weaker and poorer than it would otherwise have been. If this turns out to be the case, all sides will feel aggrieved. Some are calling for a new referendum, but if the result of a new referendum were to be as close as the last one it would settle nothing and only deepen political divisions.

In authoritarian systems, getting involved in politics is always high risk, and most citizens, believing that there is nothing much that can be done, therefore keep their heads down. Getting involved in a democratic system, in comparison, is low risk, yet still most citizens choose not to. Partly that is because of the feeling that if you get involved in politics you get tainted by it. You have to become, despite yourself, self-seeking, ruthless, and mendacious, because that is what politics everywhere requires. If you try to play by other rules, you will fail. Many people as a result drop out of politics, and cease to participate in formal politics at all. Many do not vote. They feel disengaged and estranged from politics, and are no longer concerned enough to become well informed about political issues. To the extent that they notice politics at all, it is politics as spectacle, politics as reality TV, the trivia of who's up, who's down, the clash of egos, the scandals, and the perpetual crises and panics of media politics.

Some of those who become disengaged from formal representative politics put their energies into other kinds of political involvement, community activities, and networks of various kinds. But there are a large number who disengage completely. Many young people are like this. They don't see the point of being involved. If pressed for a reason, they often say that voting doesn't change anything. The parties are all the same, and pursue the same policies when they are in government. As an old anarchist slogan said: 'Don't vote; it only encourages them.' On top of that the details of legislation or policy implementation are complex and boring. For the last two hundred years the high priests of cultural modernity have proclaimed that true self-fulfilment is to be found in the pursuit of private pleasures rather than in the performance of public service.

With the explosion of consumerism and the attraction of ideas of personal autonomy in contemporary commercial societies, everyone strives to be the architect of his or her own life. Politics is a bore and a distraction. The problem with socialism, Oscar Wilde remarked, is that it requires too many evenings. The political philosopher Richard Rorty wrote of the impossible choice for every individual between deciding when to take part in the struggle to extend social justice and when to work on their own projects. At the beginning of the modern era Voltaire depicted this dilemma in his novel *Candide*. The hero, Candide, who has a trusting, hopeful nature, is buffeted by the cruelties, selfishness, vanities, follies, and absurdities of the world, and at the end retires ruefully from the struggle to cultivate his garden. It is a path many have trodden since.

One of the strongest desires in our contemporary culture is this urge to escape from politics. There is a persistent dream of a politics-free world. Many of the greatest political thinkers in the western tradition, including Plato, Marx, and Hayek, have entertained this dream, even if they agreed on little else. To turn on the television news or access a news website is to be bombarded by a set of intractable political conflicts and policy dilemmas which often seem to have no solutions. Media presenters and bloggers routinely denounce the failure of international institutions and governments to take any decisions or initiate any actions when the world is burning (often literally) around them. A sense of fatalism, which is defined most simply as the idea that nothing will ever change and nothing will be that different, seems a rational response. Better cultivate our own garden like Candide rather than worry what is happening in countries far away of which we know little. Why bother with politics?

Can We Escape Politics?

But we can turn the question around. Why does politics as it is currently practised make us want to disengage from it, rather than to become involved and to try to understand it better? We have a pressing reason to do so if we are to limit the damage politics can do and also to unleash the potential it has to make the world a better place. Despite our desire to do so we cannot escape politics. By no means everything is political. It is only a small part of what human life is about. But it still frames everything we do. It is an ineradicable part of living together. There is politics within every human association, including families, wherever there are decisions to be made over how authority is to be justified or how resources are to be allocated, roles defined, rules formulated, and identities affirmed.

Why Bother with Politics?

Politics arises whenever there is disagreement and conflict over any of these questions.

The attraction of Daniel Defoe's story of Robinson Crusoe is that, marooned as he was on his desert island with only himself for company, he could in principle make whatever decisions he liked. There were no political constraints because there was no-one else whose agreement he had to obtain. The only constraint on the choices he could make were material – he was limited by what he could find on the island and what he managed to rescue from his wrecked ship – and psychological – his memories of how things were ordered in the society he had left, and his determination to live on the desert island as though he was still living in a human community alongside others. As soon as Man Friday enters the story, however, so too does politics, because the relationship between them has to be defined. Is it a relationship of equals in which all decisions are taken jointly, or is it a master/slave relationship in which one is subordinate to the will and decisions of the other, and carries out his commands?

Robinson Crusoe demonstrates that politics only disappears from our world under very special conditions, and quickly reappears when those conditions no longer hold. All associations and communities have their politics, but it is in the associations we call states that politics is most evident. It arises because human beings have to cooperate in order to survive, but human beings have radically different circumstances and knowledge, which means that they perceive their interests differently, form different identities, and adopt different beliefs and values. In order to cooperate, some means must be found to agree rules which can establish an order and therefore a degree of certainty and trust between the members of the association.

The power to allocate resources and determine rules in more complex associations was generally only stable if it was backed by force, and if the territorial boundaries of the association and who had a right to be considered a member were clearly defined. Who wields that power and how it is wielded are the well-springs of politics in every state, and central questions for the study of politics. It leads on to further questions. Once a common power, a state, has been established in a given territory, how is it to relate to other common powers? How such sovereign common powers recognize and interact with one another becomes another key arena for politics. Crucial also are questions of identity and belonging, who the members of the state actually are and who has the right to join or be included, and who therefore has a right to participate in the politics of the state.

Why Bother with Politics?

When Politics Goes Wrong

A second reason why we should bother with politics is that in those states where politics goes wrong, everything goes wrong. The evidence of what happens when a state collapses, when there is civil war or a natural disaster, is chilling. There is abundant evidence all around us at the present time. Take Syria. The Syrian civil war began in March 2011. As of this writing (2018) it has lasted seven long years. It was triggered by a popular uprising, part of the Arab Spring, against the authoritarian rule of Bashar al-Assad and the Ba'ath party. When the demands for peaceful change and reform were rejected by the regime, a familiar cycle developed of increasing protest and increasing repression, leading to the protesters taking up arms to overthrow their government. The war has been waged with brutality on both sides, and many outside groups have been drawn into the conflict, both jihadist groups like Daesh, who for a time occupied a great swathe of northern Syria and Iraq and proclaimed a new Caliphate, and foreign powers – the United States, France, Britain, Russia, Turkey, Iran, and Saudi Arabia.

There have been numerous horrors and atrocities – among so many the destruction of Aleppo

17

in 2017 and of Ghouta in 2018, and the use of chemical weapons, stand out, alongside Daesh's reign of terror in the areas they controlled and their attempt to blow up the ancient ruins of Palmyra because they offended their religious beliefs. Huge numbers of Syrians have been displaced, many of them forced into camps in Lebanon, Jordan, and Turkey. As many as 400,000 out of a population of 18 million may have been killed, and many more have been seriously wounded.

In its horror the Syrian war may be not very different from countless wars before it. But what is new with contemporary wars is that they are no longer far away but close at hand. The images are captured by modern media, including social media, and broadcast around the world. Large sums of aid have poured into Syria but they look insignificant in the face of the size of the catastrophe. The decision of the western powers to draw back from full intervention in 2013 was noted by Russia, which stepped up its support for the Assad regime. With Russian help, Assad seems on the brink of winning the civil war as of this writing. But Syria is in ruins: many of its cities have been completely destroyed, as has much of its infrastructure; its population has been displaced, with 500,000 refugees living outside the country unable to return; and the economy has been devastated. The Roman historian Tacitus summarized the results of one campaign by the Roman army across the Rhine into what is now Germany: 'They made a desert and called it peace.' That will be true of Syria too when the war finally ends.

Citizens of the rich democracies, used to high levels of consumption and decades of peace, feel complacent about their own societies. Many free ride. They enjoy the benefits but resent the taxes which pay for them, and look for any way they can to avoid them. But there are no guarantees that either democracy or peace is everlasting. Both can be reversed. States can break down, as the conflicts in Northern Ireland, Bosnia, Ukraine, and Syria show. If democracies are hollowed out, if international cooperation starts to break down, if new conflicts over resources start to arise, if new threats are not countered, then very quickly old questions about order and security can return. We cannot assume that the relative good fortune of some rich societies in the recent past will continue indefinitely if the political foundations which established that good fortune are neglected and allowed to waste away.

Human memory is short. Relatively soon there will be no-one alive who remembers the great wars which devastated Europe twice in successive generations in the twentieth century. Since the end of the

First World War in November 1918, the sacrifice of the millions who died has been remembered in words written specially for this purpose:

> They shall grow not old, as we that are left grow old.
> Age shall not weary them nor the years condemn.
> At the going down of the sun, and in the morning
> We will remember them.

But will we still remember them, or the dead in so many other wars, once there are no longer any survivors? The First World War killed 20 million, the Second World War 70 million. Nothing on this scale had been experienced before. The Second World War in particular involved fighting in both hemispheres and across many continents. The weapons of mass destruction, particularly nuclear weapons, which states have acquired since those conflicts mean that any future major war could potentially inflict even greater casualties, primarily on civilian populations. That is now the logic of modern war. Civilians are in the front line and are the main target.

In 1945 Hiroshima and Nagasaki in Japan were chosen as targets for the first nuclear strikes. At least 129,000 people died in the attacks. The cities were utterly destroyed. The memory of what those strikes meant for the people of those two cities has been preserved in the Peace Museum in Hiroshima, whose displays present a remarkable reconstruction of the events which led up to the bombing and a careful detailed and chilling examination of its devastating consequences. Today's nuclear bombs are many times more deadly than the bombs which struck Hiroshima and Nagasaki. But although the world understands the terrible power of these weapons, they continue to spread. More and more states want to possess them as what they imagine to be the ultimate guarantee of their security. Politics has failed so far to remove the nuclear threat from the world. But only politics can succeed in doing so. Even a limited deal like the Iran nuclear deal hard won in 2015 and casually ripped apart by President Trump in 2018 is better than the alternative. This is the paradox which will recur again and again through this book.

Everyone is born into a particular society, with its own set of laws, institutions, and circumstances. As we grow up we tend to take these for granted, as though they were 'natural', like the mountains or the oceans, since we had no part in their making. But they were made through the political activities of previous generations. It matters hugely to the quality of our lives whether we were born free or born slaves, whether we were born into a society which respects human rights or into one which does not, and what resources, opportunities, and support were available for us. The wide inequalities in the world today in the life-chances of its 7 billion people is a testament to the importance of politics, the politics which has shaped our world and the distribution of power and resources within it. Understanding how our human world has come to be what it is, and how we fit into it, is the proper study of politics. As such it is something we should all be bothered with.

In Siena there are some famous frescoes in the Council Chamber of the Town Hall. They were painted by Ambrogio Lorenzetti in 1338 and are entitled the *Allegory of Good Government* and the *Allegory of Bad Government*.[2] They depict the effects of being ruled well and being ruled badly on the lives of the citizens. In the first the people are happy and prosperous, the buildings are well maintained, and the city is flourishing. In the second the city lies in ruins, there is famine and pestilence, and

---

[2] You can see the frescoes and a detailed commentary on what they mean here: *https://flashbak.com/lorenzettis-allegory-of-good-and-bad-gov ernment-a-revolutionary-painting-for-then-and-now-373579/*. See also Patrick Boucheron, *The Power of Images: Siena, 1338*, trans. Andrew Brown (Cambridge: Polity, 2018).

rival armies are about to engage in battle. The allegories are a vivid depiction of the extent to which politics matters. Everyone is affected; everyone has a stake.

2

What is at Stake in Politics?

In recognizing that we cannot escape politics, we accept that this is because there is too much at stake in politics to ignore it. How much is readily apparent when a society breaks down, and extreme forms of politics come to dominate. But we can also grasp what is at stake in politics by studying the huge range of writing and speculation that political activities have inspired over the last three thousand years.

In the last hundred there has been an exponential growth in the number of books, articles, and newspaper columns on politics. In the last decade or so, of course, this has been accompanied by an explosion of political tweets. We are not necessarily wiser because of it. But the growth of the professional study of politics does at least alert us to the range and the complexity of the activities that can be classed as political. One of its consequences, as with many other academic disciplines, is that the study of politics has increasingly been divided into different sub-disciplines. Some of the most prominent are international relations, comparative politics, political thought, political theory, public administration, and political economy. These sub-disciplines are themselves often divided into different fields and specialisms, and new sub-disciplines are arising all the time, some of which, like gender studies, seek to overturn existing boundaries and recast the assumptions on which the study of politics has been based.

In the past, writing about politics and participating in politics was dominated by men. The classic texts of western political thought have had few prominent female authors – Mary Wollstonecraft, Ayn Rand, and Hannah Arendt stand out – and there have been few female rulers and leaders, despite some notable examples: Boudica, Cleopatra, Elizabeth I of England, and Catherine the Great of Russia. In Britain the Labour party has still not managed to elect a woman leader, although the Conservatives have had two. In most states women until very recently did not have the same civil or political rights as men. Even today there remain many obstacles, as Mary Beard points out in *Women and Power*.[1] The same is true of universities. Most teachers of political science in universities have been men, and that is reflected in the academic literature on politics. All this has begun to change quite rapidly, and many more women are being appointed to university posts and are being promoted to professorships, but there is still a long way to go.

Politics is unusual as an academic subject, at least in the UK, because the names of the departments which teach the subject can be very different. This can be confusing when you are applying to university. There are departments of political science, politics, government, international relations, politics and international studies, and several other combinations. In Sheffield the department where I obtained my first lecturing post had been named the Department of Political Theory and Institutions by its first professor, Bernard Crick. It would be easier if the profession could agree on a single name, like economics or sociology or history. But that is unlikely to happen any time soon. If you are a prospective student, the important thing to do, as with any university course, is to find out what is actually taught. When you do this, you will dis-

---

[1] Mary Beard, *Women and Power: A Manifesto* (London: Profile Books, 2017).

cover less variety. All major departments now offer a programme which includes the main sub-fields of the discipline, particularly comparative politics and international relations.

There is a reason why university departments of politics do not have a single name. Many writers on politics have observed that politics is not itself a single discipline which employs a unified method of inquiry and a common set of assumptions. Rather it is best thought of as a field of study which draws on many other disciplines to help illuminate it. These other disciplines have included philosophy, history, law, economics, sociology, psychology, as well as some disciplines in the natural sciences, such as biology. At times there have been attempts to make the study of politics much narrower by equipping it with a single methodology and perspective, banishing all the rest. But they have not succeeded, partly because of internal resistance within the profession, partly because the nature of politics itself defies the attempts to imprison it.

The study of politics is much better approached through the questions which reverberate through both the practice of politics and the study of it. They are questions which have preoccupied some of the greatest political thinkers, such as Plato, Hobbes, Rousseau, and Marx, thinkers important in their own time and still read today, long after most of their contemporaries have been forgotten. If we want to understand their thought in any depth, we need to study what they had to say in the context of their time, and look at the arguments their contemporaries were making and to which they were often responding. This is the historical approach, pioneered in particular by Michael Oakeshott, Quentin Skinner, and John Dunn. But it is also legitimate to consider the greatest thinkers from a philosophical standpoint, analysing their arguments separately from their historical context. One of the great exponents of this method was Isaiah Berlin. Approaching the classic texts through the questions which preoccupied these thinkers is a very good way of appreciating the range and diversity of politics, and of starting to study the subject. It arouses interest in the big questions of politics and the diversity of responses to them, and lays the groundwork for more advanced study of the texts themselves. I have chosen five of these big questions (there are many others) to illustrate this.

How is Order Possible?

The first question is the most basic. Under what circumstances do free, prosperous, and orderly human societies emerge? No-one wants to live in fear of their life or in fear of being robbed. Human beings crave the certainty of an order which protects their lives and their possessions and allows them to live without constant anxiety that the things they most value might at any moment be snatched away. Two broad answers have been given to this question. There are those like the eighteenth-century French political philosopher Jean-Jacques Rousseau, who argued in *The Social Contract* that men are born free but are everywhere in chains. Human beings are naturally cooperative and peaceful, but they are corrupted and enslaved by societies. If the spontaneous goodness of human nature can be liberated, human beings will establish orderly and peaceful societies without the need for coercion or violence. The other view, associated with Thomas Hobbes among others, is that human beings are naturally violent, self-interested, and rapacious, so unless they are restrained by a higher power they will seek to plunder and subjugate one another.

What is striking about both ways of posing the question is that the answer is the same – the state. But it is a very different kind of state, as we shall see. Anarchist thinkers from the anarcho-communist Peter Kropotkin to the anarcho-capitalist Murray Rothbard reject the state altogether, arguing that it will always take away freedom and become oppressive, and that human beings do not need the state to form cooperative communities. A contemporary take on this is the idea that digital democracy offers a way to dispense with representative government, the whole apparatus of parliaments and elected politicians, by allowing the people to control government directly through daily plebiscites. But most writers on politics, whatever their view of human nature, see the state as an essential institution to guarantee order, at least in the period since human beings emerged from being nomadic hunter gatherers, and established agriculture, settled communities, and cities, some five thousand years ago.

Today the state is everywhere. Could we imagine modern life without it? We bump into the state at every turn. It registers our births, our marriages, our deaths. It provides education and health; it builds roads and airports. It regulates what we eat and drink; it issues us with driving licences when we want to drive and passports when we want to travel abroad; it imprisons us when we break its laws; and it collects taxes from us to pay for all its activities on our behalf. The state is omnipresent and can seem omnipotent, towering over the individual, who is helpless before it. This new reality is powerfully explored in the writing of Franz Kafka and

George Orwell. In the modern world it has become necessary to be a citizen of a particular state. Some people manage to be a citizen of more than one state at the same time. What no-one can afford to be is 'stateless', because that means you lose your rights and your identity. There is no state to protect you, and you have no right to live anywhere. Everyone has to be assigned to a state, which is then assumed to have a duty to protect its citizens, but also has the power to monitor and control them.

The fact that we have come to rely on the state to provide order and certainty in our lives should not blind us to what an unusual idea this is. The idea of the modern state has not always existed. One version first emerged in the sixteenth and seventeenth centuries in Europe, although there are earlier antecedents, particularly in the Islamic world. What distinguished it from earlier forms of political association and made it 'modern' was that the state gradually came to be understood as a form of public power separate from both ruler and ruled and constituting the supreme political authority within a defined territory. In the past the state had often been inseparable from the person of the ruler. Once a distinction was made between the state as a form of public power and the ruler, it meant that rulers could in principle be held accountable to the laws enacted by the state. Being the ruler was a public office like any other. The idea that no-one is above the law, and that the existence of the state is not tied to any particular individual or family, was a turning point in how the state in Europe developed. Among other things it opened the way to representative forms of government, the rise of independent courts, and freedom of speech and association.

Once the state is conceived as a form of public power, a host of other questions arise. Firstly, how is this power organized? What are the institutions and agencies through which it is expressed? What are the purposes of the state? Secondly, what makes this power legitimate? How is this public power accountable to the citizens for its actions? Thirdly, how are the boundaries of the state set? How is its territory to be defined, and how are disputes with other states over these boundaries to be resolved?

If the state as a public power separate from rulers and ruled comes to be seen as the main guarantor of order, then it allows the purposes of the state to be thought about in many different ways. Some have stressed that the main purpose of the state is government – the enactment and enforcement of laws to keep citizens safe. The state arises out of the willingness of citizens to form an association to empower a government. Such a state claims a particular territory as its own and seeks to control who may cross its borders. Every state appears distinct, with its own characteristics and idiosyncrasies. At times state and society appear to merge, forming a complex whole. The state becomes the society it represents. State and society are not the same, but sometimes we speak as though they were. We speak of France, and we mean the population, resources, organizations, capacities, institutions, and culture of that country. The French state embodies them. As General de Gaulle, President of France from 1959 to 1969, expressed it: 'Toute ma vie je me suis fait une certaine idée de la France.' ('All my life I have had a certain idea of France')

From another angle the state is only one association among many. It has its uses, but it is also a danger to the rest of society and needs to be watched constantly so that its power does not grow. As a public power, the state is a legal organization, a set of agencies and institutions, and it claims a monopoly within that society of the means of violence and rule making. It is the leading association, the one which guarantees the rights and safety of all the others, but it does not absorb all other associations, some of which may be better expressions of the national community. In this tradition the state is often seen negatively, as a destructive and violent force. Its bias is always to intervene too much, seeking to control the lives of its citizens in too many details and to reorganize all other associations in ways that conform to its preferences.

These two different ways of thinking about the state are sometimes called society-centred and state-centred accounts. What is at stake is whether we think of the state as an agent, with autonomy, will, and purpose, able to shape events and outcomes, or whether we think of it as just a cipher, the outward expression of more fundamental forces which are the real drivers of social change. Can the state act, and what does it mean to say that it can? The state is made up a multitude of agencies and institutions, employing millions of individuals. Is anyone in charge of these vast bureaucratic structures? Is it right to attribute to the state a will and purpose? Some have argued that the state is simply an arena, a space where classes, interests, and groups battle for supremacy. What the state does reflects the balance of these social forces. A similar view is that the state should be thought of not as an actor but as a network between organizations which are dependent upon one another for resources. What we call the state is a constant process of negotiation and coordination between different parts of that network.

The contrary view emphasizes that the state is primarily a legitimate order, which claims authority over the community. Citizens are obliged to obey the commands of the state if they are issued in a legal manner. So long as it is constituted according to law and acts according to law, the state embodies legitimate authority and the identity of the community and has to be obeyed. Some then take this further and argue that the state can also be an enterprise which can attempt to lead society in a particular direction, reforming institutions, giving priority to particular goals, using its authority to ensure certain outcomes. One of the enterprises for which modern states have been notorious is war, and war has been a great shaper of the modern state, one of the drivers of its growth. To defend themselves and to expand, states have needed large armies and navies, and that helped spur the economic development to create the military hardware and the human resources to support great military adventures.

We do not need to choose between these perspectives. As often in the study of politics, both give us insights into how states are. All states in our time are embodiments and expressions of their communities, and the balance of interests and cultures within them, yet they also seek to lead and shape them. One reason we are confused by the modern state is that it is necessarily both these things. Another reason is because the state has grown so big. Modern states have acquired enormous reach and control over their societies and over their neighbourhoods; they have capacities which earlier states could not imagine.

The most absolute rulers of the past could exercise power within their courts and their capital but often struggled to exercise control over remote regions because of the distances involved and the poor quality of communications and transport. In large states it could take weeks or months for messages to be received. Local rulers and commanders had high levels of autonomy. All that has changed in the modern world as distances have shrunk and modern communications allow immediate contact all around the world. You have to travel to the remotest parts of the planet to escape the reach of the modern state.

Who Gets What, When, and How?

Once order is achieved and a state established, a key question for politics in that state is how power and wealth are distributed. The American political scientist Harold Lasswell summed up the question as 'who gets what, when, how'.[2] Roman judges used to put a blunt question in criminal trials, 'Cui bono?' To whom is it a benefit? For Lenin the question was about the struggle for supremacy between classes and between social systems. He posed it in 1921 as 'Who will overtake whom?' This was shortened to 'Who/Whom?' ('Kto-Kovo?') Who wins and who loses in the competition for wealth and power turns on the rules which are established or confirmed through politics. These rules embody one of the three social mechanisms through which complex societies are coordinated: hierarchies, markets, and networks.

Hierarchies are most visible in large top-down organizations. There are some people at the top and many more at the bottom, and others at different levels in between. Think of government departments, or large corporations, or universities, or churches. What they all have in common is that power has been centralized so that a few individuals at the apex have the authority to take decisions on behalf of the organization, and receive much greater rewards and privileges, material and non-material,

[2] Harold D. Lasswell, *Politics: Who Gets What, When, How* (New York: Peter Smith, 1936).

for doing so. They have bigger offices, chauffeur-driven cars, bigger salaries, and better pensions, for example. They also have varying degrees of control over those lower down in the hierarchy. At its extreme this means that a decision at the top is passed down the chain of command and has to be obeyed by everyone further down. If it is not obeyed or implemented, there can be sanctions against subordinates.

This model is a military one; it is how armies are supposed to perform. In practice very few hierarchies, even military ones, come close to this. There is always a problem of compliance and implementation. This has always been the subject of satire, as in the British sitcoms *Yes Minister* and *Yes Prime Minister*. Someone at the top of a hierarchy can issue a command or pull a lever, but subordinates lower down the hierarchy may not choose to implement it, or implement it only partially. This is either because they do not understand the command, or because it is too difficult, or because they are too busy with other things or have other priorities, or because in some circumstances they think the command is absurd, or wrong, and they actively subvert it. Such active resistance is uncommon – there are powerful sanctions against it – but it still takes place. Such people are sometimes called whistleblowers.

What is at Stake in Politics?

Computer analyst Edward Snowden in 2013 copied and then leaked thousands of documents from the US National Security Agency (NSA), revealing the existence of many secret global surveillance programmes run by the NSA and European governments. He then fled to Russia to avoid arrest. He has always insisted that his purpose was to alert his fellow citizens to what was being done in their name and the extent of the surveillance which the state had authorized on its own citizens without their knowledge. His protest was aimed at power which had become unaccountable, but as a result of his actions he faces a long prison sentence if he ever returns to the United States or if Russia ceases to protect him.

We are very familiar with hierarchies. Much of our common social life is organized through them. What hierarchies do is define for each member of the hierarchy a particular status. That status prescribes rights and duties, and it bestows privileges and resources. Individuals often feel comfortable within hierarchies because the clear expectations of the role they must play give them a degree of security so long as they conform and act out that role. In some hierarchies individuals are able to start at the bottom and work their way up to the top. There is, however, not room at the top for everyone. Only one person at a time can be the Prime Minister of the UK, the President of China, the Vice Chancellor of Oxford, the Supreme Leader of Iran, the CEO of the Red Cross, the Archbishop of Canterbury, the CEO of Microsoft, or the UN Secretary-General.

Many hierarchies in democracies have become more open than they were. Traditional hierarchies were often closed. Status was determined by birth, and many positions in the hierarchy could only be occupied by those who had the right line of descent. When the French Revolution declared that all careers, particularly those in the army, should be open to everyone and that the criterion of advancement should be talent rather than birth, what you could do rather than who you were, it was a revolutionary principle whose reverberations are still being felt. But it has taken a very long time in practice for many hierarchies to be reformed.

Another way that status was assigned was on grounds of gender. Most Christian churches have until very recently refused to allow women to be ordained as priests. Several professions and clubs had a bar on women. Even when these were relaxed it has still taken a very long time for women to rise to the top of many hierarchies in any considerable numbers. One hundred years since votes for women were won in most democracies, recent campaigns on pay and sexual harassment have highlighted how little progress there has been in some core areas in achieving gender equality. Not only have many fewer women than men risen to the top of hierarchies in politics, business, the media, the arts, and science, but scandalously many women have been paid less than their male counterparts even when they have been doing the same job.

Markets are different. They coordinate human activities not through a hierarchy of command but through exchange between individuals. The principle of such exchanges is that the parties to the exchange offer something which the other wants, so there is a mutual benefit, and both feel satisfied. The exchange can involve tangible things. You have some apples, more than you can eat yourself, and I have an extra loaf of bread. We exchange and both benefit. It can also involve services. I agree to spend my time working for you, and in return you pay me a wage. In their origins markets were local and involved face-to-face contact, and often forms of barter. As they expanded and became more complex, barter proved inefficient, and forms of money emerged. Everything of practical use to anyone else could be given a value in whatever commodity came to be used as money. This allowed an enormous expansion of the geographical reach and the internal complexity of markets. They extended ultimately to the whole world.

Hierarchies tend to concentrate power; markets tend to disperse it, but only so long as there are many suppliers of each particular commodity in the market, and if all the participants in the market are roughly equal in terms of their initial endowments of skills and resources. In practice this is rarely achieved. The circumstances of individuals in market economies are very different. Some have great initial advantages: the families they are born into, the education and healthcare they receive, the assets which are at their disposal. The majority start out with very little. They only have their labour power to sell.

For a market economy to work in the ideal way imagined by its strongest advocates, there would need to be what has been called 'starting-gate equality'. Everyone as far as possible should begin with the same opportunities and endowments. But because endowments and opportunities are not equal, market outcomes are often skewed, and lead to persistent and structural problems of inequality. The ownership of property and assets has always been highly concentrated, and this determines the life chances of everyone. In this way markets themselves become hierarchies and reinforce the hierarchies in social institutions. A few individuals are able to break free from their initial position and create great wealth, which then may assist them in gaining high status as well.

The rise of market economies has undermined the closed nature of many hierarchies, but it has by no means eliminated them. When hierarchies and markets combine, the result is what we call capitalism. In the modern world, who gets what, when, and how is determined in every society by the particular kind of capitalism that has been established, the particular mix of state and market, of hierarchy and exchange.

The third method of coordinating human societies is networks. They also involve exchange but money is not involved. Traditional networks include families and communities. The traditional bonds that tie people together are kinship and neighbourhood. But as the scale of society has grown through the enlargement of hierarchies and markets, so networks have grown too. Networks intersect with both markets and hierarchies. The rules governing markets and hierarchies are formal and explicit, but the rules governing networks are informal and often tacit.

Many professions in the modern world are organized as networks, some of which are global in scope.

Scientists are part of a world-wide community, connected through the exchange of information, results, and ideas through the networks which they establish. Academic journals and international conferences play a key part in organizing such networks. Religions, although they have their hierarchical aspects, also tend to function as networks. People of the same faith find one another through them. The diaspora of ethnic groups around the world also creates networks which immigrants make use of to get support. Networks tend to be altruistic and cooperative rather than self-interested and competitive. They are held together by some common experience, common circumstance, or common interest.

The character of the markets, the hierarchies, and the networks in any society, and the way in which they combine to form particular institutions, are crucial for determining the life chances of its members, in determining who gets what, when, and how. Politics plays a big part in shaping those institutions. What is at stake is the inequality between human beings, the extent of discrimination against individuals because of their gender, ethnicity, age, class, or religion. How power is exercised and in whose interests has always been at the centre of politics.

In many traditional pre-modern societies inequality became entrenched, with permanent hereditary aristocracies and dynasties, which solidified their power through making sharp distinctions between the status of different groups, as in the Indian caste system. In modern societies the boundaries between groups have become more fluid, aided by democratic and egalitarian doctrines which have asserted that all human beings should be treated the same. But marked inequalities persist, some of them arising from institutional hierarchies, others from the way in which capitalist markets work. The latter tend to lead to very wide inequalities in income and wealth which then become consolidated in the unequal status of families, the passing on of advantage through the networks of kinship.

Who Should Rule and How Should They Rule?

The existence of a state means that power has been centralized within a community. How centralized such a power is can vary, but at the very least a means will have been established for taking authoritative decisions which are binding for everyone who is a member of the state. Once there is such a common power the question becomes how it should be constituted, whether it should be unconstrained or held in check, and who should wield it. Much ink and much blood has been spilled over these questions. Who has the authority to take decisions on behalf of the political community? Legitimate authority can be established in many ways. It can belong to an absolute monarch whose authority is derived from God, or it can be legitimate because in some sense it represents all the interests of the community, so that no-one is overlooked when crucial decisions are taken.

Theories of representative government have laid great emphasis on the need to ensure that the interests and identities of all citizens are accommodated and respected. If this is not the case, the ruling power may come to be perceived as acting against the interests of some members or even a majority of the community, leading to political resistance, rebellion, or even revolution. In January 1917, just before the revolution which toppled the Romanov dynasty in Russia, the British Ambassador requested an audience with the Tsar, Nicholas II. The authority of the Government had broken down, significant sections of the army had mutinied, and the streets of St Petersburg were filled with workers and soldiers demanding change. The British Ambassador ventured to suggest that, given the situation, it might be appropriate for the Tsar to take steps to regain the confidence of his people. The Tsar replied that, on the contrary, it was for his people to take steps to regain *his* confidence.

Thomas Hobbes argued in *Leviathan* that so long as the sovereign maintained order and civil peace, citizens had a duty to obey the sovereign's commands, no matter how capricious, cruel, arbitrary, or oppressive those commands were. Hobbes was shaped by his experience of the English civil war. Anything was better than the destruction and violence of a civil war. If a sovereign power arose which could bring it to an end, that made it legitimate. This was not an abstract theoretical question for Hobbes. He acted on his own argument. He had supported the King in the civil war and went into exile when the King was defeated. But once Charles had been executed and Oliver Cromwell had become the new ruler of the country, Hobbes accepted that there was a new sovereign power, which it was his duty to obey. So he returned to England. His employers, the Cavendish family, forgave him, but many Royalists never did, and following the restoration of the monarchy after Cromwell's death Hobbes' books were burned in the marketplace in Cambridge.

Not many have followed Hobbes all the way in

his reasoning, because they dislike his conclusion: that tyranny and despotic rule are a price worth paying for civil peace. His critics argued that it was possible to preserve peace by a government that was limited, subject to the rule of law, and accountable to its citizens. If a government was despotic, citizens had a right to resist and rebel, and change the sovereign. This argument was made by John Locke in opposing the increasingly despotic rule of the English Stuart Kings Charles II and his brother James II. James was overthrown in the Glorious Revolution of 1688, and a much more limited monarchy was installed. This lesson was studied by the American colonists and used as a justification for their own rebellion against the British King which led to the American Revolution and the founding of the United States on republican principles. A constitution was adopted to limit executive power so that no despotic sovereign like George III could arise within the United States.

One of the slogans of the American Revolution was no taxation without representation. The colonists had many grievances, but one of the main ones was that they were taxed by the Westminster Parliament, but they had no representation in it, and so no say over the laws it passed or over the policy of the British Government. It became a fundamental principle of the liberal tradition of representative government that governments had to be limited, representative, and accountable. That was not the same as being democratic. That came later. The US Constitution was designed to frustrate democracy not enable it. In their republican vision of what good government entailed they wanted to avoid the tyranny of an absolutist ruler but also the tyranny of the mob. For the Founding Fathers democracy was very definitely associated with the latter. That is why they went to such trouble to ensure that the US President would not be directly elected by the people, but only indirectly by the Senate, fearing otherwise the rise of populists and demagogues who would subvert the Republic.

The argument between Hobbes and his critics turns on whether it is ever acceptable for the sovereign to act despotically. For Hobbes it is a false argument. The sovereign has to act despotically to disarm the citizens and ensure civil peace. Whenever there are national emergencies, for example a terrorist attack, or an external threat of invasion, the Government acts despotically and often outside the rule of law to ensure the safety of the citizens and to protect the national territory. If the sovereign power is not prepared to act despotically, it ceases to be sovereign. Against threats to the existence of the state itself the sovereign cannot afford to consult or represent or seek consensus. It has to act, and act decisively.

This dilemma is a deeply troubling one, and one which has become still more intense with the advent of nuclear weapons. In the Cuban missile crisis in 1962, the decision whether or not to take immediate action to destroy the missile sites in Cuba which the Soviet Union had established and risk the possibility of a full nuclear exchange between the two superpowers had to be taken by the US President, John F. Kennedy. It could not have been decided by waiting for Congress to deliberate or for the public to form a view. Despite the urging of many of his military advisers to take out the missile sites, Kennedy chose to delay and instead issued an ultimatum to the Soviet President, Nikita Khruschchev, that the USSR must halt the convoy which was on its way with more missiles and supplies for the sites, and must undertake to dismantle them.

After a tense stand-off an agreement was hammered out which gave the Americans what they wanted. The Soviets agreed to dismantle the missile sites, in return for the US guaranteeing that it would not invade Cuba, and pledging to dismantle its own missile sites in Turkey, which were as close to the Soviet Union as the Cuban missiles were to the

United States. This concession was kept secret and only revealed much later. The crisis was defused, but only just. It showed the importance of the character of the leaders involved in such situations, in this case Kennedy and Khrushchev. With different leaders the outcome might have been otherwise. Politics mattered.

What Stops States Fighting One Another?

This example leads directly into the next question: the problem of order in the international state system. If there is not one global sovereign, but many individual sovereigns, all with their own territories, their own interests, their own identities, how is war to be prevented? If the natural human condition is the war of all against all, which can only be held in check by a sovereign, then since the international state system lacks a single sovereign, it seems destined to be always in a state of perpetual war rather than perpetual peace.

Yet although it is possible to see human history as little more than a succession of wars between states seeing to maximize their wealth, power, and territory, this is only partially true. For long periods states have shown the capacity to live in peace and even cooperate with other states. Even if this does not amount to the perpetual peace which the philosopher Immanuel Kant advocated, it is still far short of perpetual war. An international state system has evolved in which all states acknowledge certain rules of behaviour in their dealings with one another. Since the advent of the democratic era it is a remarkable and rather surprising fact that no two democracies have gone to war with one another, although they have fought many wars against authoritarian and despotic regimes, most notably Nazi Germany. The main reason appears to be that there are other ways to reconcile their differences, and the need to win over public opinion for a war policy sets limits to the influence of the war party. Citizens of western democracies have become increasingly unwilling to serve and risk their lives in war or to have others do it in their name.

Power and the pursuit of national interest remain, however, as core aspects of the international state system, so it is not surprising that some analysts see little else. One of the most chilling passages ever written about international relations is the reconstruction by Thucydides in his *History of the Peloponnesian War* of the negotiations between the Athenians and the Melians in the fifth century BCE. Athens was a mighty empire and Melos was a small island which was neutral in the conflict between Athens and Sparta. Neutral, that is, until the day an Athenian fleet appeared off the island. The Athenians had a simple request. They invited the Melians to abandon their neutrality and form an alliance with Athens.

The Melians considered the request and politely declined it. The Athenians immediately changed their tone. You don't understand, they told the Melians. You are not in a position to decline our request. If you refuse to ally with us and join the war with Sparta, we will attack you, destroy your city, and enslave all your people. We have more power than you and therefore you must do as we say. The weak must always bend to the strong. On hearing this ultimatum the Melians still refused to form an alliance with Athens. The city was besieged and captured, the men killed, and the women and children enslaved.

This example has always been cited as a perfect illustration of the logic of power politics. Against those who have more power than you have, resistance can seem futile. That is why in international politics many countries seek the protection of a more powerful ally to counter the threat from other states, as Cuba did with the Soviet Union, or South Korea did with the United States. We remain far from achieving any kind of single political or ideological community which could form the basis for global governance and make it legitimate.

The biggest strides towards global governance and the institutions of a global state have come from the increasing interdependence of the international economy. The World Trade Organization, the International Monetary Fund, and the World Bank are three such institutions which have arisen to govern and regulate an international economy which remains split between numerous competing national jurisdictions. The efforts of the United Nations to reduce conflict between states by referring disputes to the Security Council has been less successful, because the major powers, the victors of the Second World War, who became the permanent members of the Security Council after 1945, generally pursue their own national interests, and veto resolutions whenever these conflict with them.

What is at stake in international relations is the peace of the world, and the ability of nations to live without being threatened by their more powerful neighbours. Despite its many failures, of which Syria is the latest example, as well as one of the most harrowing, the UN still exists more than seventy years since it was founded. Its predecessor, the League of Nations, did not last two decades, and was hampered from the start by the refusal of the US Congress to ratify the deal which President Woodrow Wilson had worked so hard to achieve. Since 1945 there has not been a major war between the great powers. The Cuban missile crisis is the closest the world has been to that.

Some argue there has been no major war because of the advent of nuclear weapons, which have raised the stakes involved much higher than they have ever been. The threatened destruction of all the major cities and much of the population of a country is too devastating to contemplate. Others have suggested that growing economic integration is another reason, particularly following the demise of the Soviet Union, and the entry of China and India as full participants in the international economy. Trade in the past has been a weapon of war as well as a facilitator of peace and could become so again. But it reduces the attraction of reverting to a zero-sum world. Preserving the kind of international order which has emerged since 1945, even with all its imperfections, is an objective of much international politics and diplomacy. Many multilateral (the word means literally many-sided) agreements, such as the Paris Agreement on climate change, which have underpinned and advanced international order and cooperation are under threat right now from the rise of aggressive nationalism around the world. The spectre of the wars, both economic and military, which engulfed the fragile international order of the 1920s and 1930s is a standing reminder of what is at stake.

Who Are Our Friends and Who Are Our Enemies?

One of the things which binds human beings together is a sense of identity and belonging which is rooted in an experience of a particular place and being brought up in a particular culture. These provide some of our deepest emotional attachments. They form the basis for allegiance to particular groups and associations and are a crucial underpinning for the cohesion and legitimacy of states. States persist not only when they serve their members' interests but also when they are an expression of their identity. That sense of who we are is one of the most powerful in politics. It is also one of the most divisive, since a large part in determining who we are is defining who we are not. One of the great driving forces in politics is distinguishing friends from enemies. Margaret Thatcher's enquiry about a member of her own party, 'Is he one of us?', is a seminal question which occurs in political parties and governments everywhere. People look for signs that someone is like them, from the same background and culture, committed to the same causes, holding the same beliefs.

Much of this process of differentiating ourselves and determining who we are is benign. It is when identities become exclusive and people feel threatened by the presence of others they regard as not belonging that fear and insecurity can breed hatred and violence. Politics can bring people together through dialogue and negotiation. It can also polarize them, and inflame tensions and deepen divides. Deciding that those who are different from you are not just different but hostile or even evil has led to some of the darkest moments in human history, and brings us up against the stubborn facts of human hatreds.

These hatreds are clear enough in outbreaks of intercommunal strife as in India and Pakistan in 1947, in Bosnia in the 1990s, in Rwanda in 1995, in Armenia in 1915, and in Northern Ireland in the 1970s. Some of the hardest events to understand are situations as in Bosnia where families of different ethnic groups, in that case Serbs and Muslims, had been living together in the same communities for generations, yet when the violence started some of these former neighbours committed unspeakable crimes against each other. The sudden switch from a society which had been living in peace and in which any ethnic tensions were contained to one where communities terrorized one another and people had to flee for their lives has been repeated in many places.

When divisions become this intense, political leaders inevitably emerge who claim to represent their community and use extremist language to mobilize support. If such politicians gain the upper hand, then the divisions become a chasm, and if they can lay hands on the machinery of the state, then the state can itself be used to persecute minorities and build walls. States have pursued policies of ethnic cleansing, which involve the attempted removal of a particular ethnic minority from a territory, and policies of genocide, which involve intentional killing. Arno Mayer entitled his book on the Holocaust 'Why did the heavens not darken?' in response to the planned murder by the Nazis of 6 million Jews.[3]

But what perhaps is really shocking about the Holocaust is what Hannah Arendt, commenting on the trial of Adolf Eichmann, called 'the banality of

---

[3] Arno J. Mayer, *Why Did the Heavens Not Darken? The 'Final Solution' in History* (London: Verso, 1990).

evil'.[4] By this she meant that Eichmann, at his 1961 trial in Jerusalem for Nazi war crimes, appeared as a normal person, not a psychopath. He denied responsibility for his actions, maintaining that he had simply been doing his duty and following orders as an official in the German state. Arendt drew attention to the willingness of individuals to commit horrendous acts if required to do so by a higher authority. This was also the chilling finding of the Milgram study at Yale in the early 1960s which showed that almost two-thirds of student volunteers were prepared to follow instructions and administer what they thought were severe electric shocks to learners rather than challenge the authority of the researchers.

The Wannsee conference in 1942, chaired by SS General Reinhard Heydrich, brought together specialists across the German Government and German military – lawyers, diplomats, engineers, scientists, and planners – to discuss how to implement a Europe-wide final solution of the Jewish question. Eichmann ordered that all transcripts of the discussions should be destroyed, but one copy survived. What we learn from it is how these high officials in

---

4 Hannah Arendt, *Eichmann in Jerusalem: A Report on the Banality of Evil* (London: Penguin, 1976).

the Nazi regime discussed the proposed elimination of 6 million people as a technical issue. What would be the most effective way of killing such numbers of people? How were Jewish people to be defined? Did having one Jewish grandfather make you eligible for the gas chambers? What were the logistics and the security aspects involved in transporting such large numbers of people from all across Europe to the camps? How could the purpose of the camps be disguised? At no point did anyone make any moral objection to what was being proposed, or register the enormity of what they were discussing. Instead it was treated as just another bureaucratic project which needed to be planned and implemented in the most efficient and expeditious way possible.

Some of the specific forms which modern racism has taken were made possible by the modern state and its greatly extended reach and capacity to monitor and control its citizens and to organize and execute great enterprises. Antisemitism existed for many centuries in Europe, and there were pogroms against the Jews in many European cities, and some mass expulsions, as in England in the thirteenth century and Spain two centuries later. But the impetus to purify nations came from nineteenth-century nationalist and racial doctrines in Europe. A key role was played by political elites and political movements. The Jewish Museum in Berlin traces in great detail the history of the Jewish community in Germany and shows how integrated into German society Jews had become by the 1920s, although many still faced discrimination.

The decision by the Nazi Government first to take away their civil and political rights, then to attempt to expel them, finally to transport them to the camps and murder them, was based on the nationalist and racial doctrines which had acquired such a hold on part of the German population, and in part explains why so many German citizens remained passive as the campaign against the Jews gathered strength. Jews were depicted as evil and implacably hostile to German national identity. They had to be removed if German nationality was not to be corrupted. It is hard to relate the hate propaganda against the Jews orchestrated by the Nazis to the images in the Jewish Museum of the normal and thoroughly German family and working lives of Jews in Germany before 1933.

But it would be wrong to end on too pessimistic a note. Although major disasters like the Nazi Holocaust or Stalin's Great Terror in the 1930s, the killing fields of Cambodia's Pol Pot in the 1970s, or the Rwandan genocide in the 1990s might make us despair of politics and the evil it can do, there is a more hopeful side. Politics can also initiate peace processes which try to bring communities together after bitter conflict, as in South Africa and Northern Ireland in the 1990s. The point about a peace process is that the two sides are not expected to like one another. What is aimed at is truth and reconciliation, bringing former enemies together, acknowledging crimes, and trying to create a new basis for cooperation and mutual respect. In some countries this has involved innovative forms of power sharing, so that both communities feel respected, treated equally, and given a say in government. The trick is to break cycles of conflict and violence and create in their place cycles of cooperation and peace. Rodney King was an African-American whose savage beating by Los Angeles police in 1991 following a high-speed car chase was caught on video, which then went viral. The officers responsible were put on trial but acquitted. That verdict sparked six days of rioting which cost many lives and caused much destruction. From his hospital bed King issued an appeal for calm which contained the memorable lines, 'Can we all get along? ... We're all stuck here for a while, let's, you know, let's try to work it out, let's try to beat it, you know, let's try to work it out.'

Politics can drive people apart but it can also bring them together. That is what is at stake.

3

What is the Point of Studying Politics?

There may be a lot at stake in politics and it may be that we cannot escape politics even if we wanted to, but what is the point of studying it? Would it not be better just to engage in it? In Goethe's play *Faust*, Mephistopheles tells Faust, 'All theory, my friend, is grey, but green is life's glad golden tree.' The young Karl Marx wrote in his *Theses on Feuerbach*, 'Philosophers have only interpreted the world in various ways; the point is to change it.' Faust was damned and Marx spent more of his life in the British Museum Reading Room studying and writing rather than actively engaging in politics. He fretted that the revolution he expected might break out before he had had time to complete his master-work, *Das Kapital*.

Others have wondered if the subject matter of politics has become too vast and too complex for anyone to get their heads around. If politics is a field of study rather than a discipline, does this not make it a very difficult subject to study at university? Would it not be better to study a subject which has a single disciplinary basis and clear boundaries? If the subject matter is so diffuse and broad, and the potential methods of analysis so numerous, is it possible to gain any real knowledge of politics? Studying politics can certainly be challenging, but fortunately the body of scholarship and methods that have been built up over many generations make the task manageable. You cannot cover everything in a Politics course at university, but then that is true of all subjects. What a Politics course equips you with are ways of thinking about politics, and tools for analysing a wide range of political problems and events.

Politics and Truth

But can the study of politics be objective? Politics as an activity has always had a difficult relationship with truth. In the eyes of many voters politicians routinely lie and dissemble. Is it possible to pierce the fog? If those who study politics possess an expertise on which everyone can rely, is it possible to be objective about politics, and stand outside it in making judgements about it? Or is truth in politics always relative, defined by power? Why else do contemporary politicians put such effort and resources into 'spin', trying to control the 'narrative', the way stories are reported and for how long?

Humpty Dumpty makes the point in a sharp exchange with Alice in *Through the Looking-Glass*: '"When I use a word," Humpty Dumpty said in a rather scornful tone, "it means just what I choose it to mean – neither more nor less." "The question is," said Alice, "whether you *can* make words mean so many very different things." "The question is," said Humpty Dumpty, "which is to be master, that's all."' He echoes the wry observation of the Tudor courtier Sir John Harrington: 'Treason doth never thrive. What's the reason? For if it thrive none dare call it treason.'

We live in an era of fake news and alternative facts. Increasing attempts are being made using electronic media to launch false news stories, targeting those whose profile suggests they might be influenced in how they vote by stories with a particular slant. When accused of using banks of computers to spread lies and disinformation in a bid to disrupt elections in western democracies and influence their outcome, the Russian Government denied all knowledge and intent. Donald Trump repeatedly makes claims that no-one else thinks are true, apart from his hapless Press Secretary, who is paid to believe them and defend them. One of the cornerstones of republican government is that politicians are honest and can be relied on to tell the truth, and if they are found to have lied and misled their colleagues and the public, they should resign. Trump operates to a different code. If you shout loud enough, he thinks, your version of events will define the political reality. Your base will rally round you, and your opponents will be wrongfooted and unable effectively to counter your lies or prove you are lying.

Worries about media and their effect upon the way politics is conducted are not new. Different kinds of media, and, particularly, innovative ones, have always been seen as potential threats to maintaining the integrity of the public sphere. Countering them is the responsibility of elected politicians and responsible media proprietors. But what is to be done when the President of the Republic himself appears to believe that politics is a branch of the entertainment industry, a live reality TV show, in which truth and responsibility matter much less than creating drama and feeding resentments?

Trump boasted that the crowds on his

Inauguration Day were bigger than the crowds for Barack Obama. A trivial issue in itself, it quickly became a symbol of the Trump Presidency and its relationship to the truth. Video footage which convinced impartial observers indicated quite clearly that Trump was wrong. Instead of backing down gracefully, however, he doubled down, repeated the original boast, and accused the media of faking the evidence which showed anything to the contrary. This was a candidate who got his doctor during the election campaign to issue a statement extolling his health, declaring that it was 'astonishingly excellent' and that his physical strength and stamina were 'extraordinary'. The letter continued, 'If elected, Mr Trump, I can state unequivocally, will be the healthiest individual ever elected to the presidency.' In April 2018 the doctor, Max Bornstein, revealed that he was not responsible for the contents of the letter. The words had been supplied by Trump himself.

All politicians seek to manage their image, and ensure that good things are said about them. But in a reality TV world all truth becomes relative. Anything can be asserted, however outrageous, and if repeated often enough many may come to accept it as the truth, because they want it to be the truth. For this approach to be successful, any independent objective or impartial opinion has to be denigrated, as well as any kind of independent expertise, because otherwise they would place limits on the messages that could be sent out. Trump's position, and that of many populist nationalists in other countries, is that all opinions and beliefs are equally valid and equally fallacious. What counts is who can seize control of the narrative and assert a line vigorously, unrelentingly, and shamelessly.

When the western powers accused Syria of using chemical weapons in attacks on its own people in April 2018, the Russians intervened and categorically rebutted every claim. The evidence collected on the site showing that the injuries suffered by children in the hospital were consistent with the use of chemical weapons was dismissed with the counter-charge that the evidence must have been faked by those making the allegation. In such a topsy-turvy world it is hard to keep your footing. Polls showed that a large majority of the Russian people believed that their leaders were telling the truth and that the charges were fake and malicious inventions of Russia's enemies. Is studying politics like this? Is objectivity completely impossible? Should we just accept that all we are doing in studying politics is reinforcing our own opinions and prejudices?

The belief that substantial objectivity is possible

both in the study and in the practice of politics is indispensable to the building of a strong civil and political order. Lies have to be rebutted. In 1937 Hitler's planes supporting Franco's Nationalist army in the Spanish civil war attacked the Basque town of Gernica.[1] The Basque region around Bilbao was a centre of Republican resistance to the Spanish Fascists and had a special significance as it was also the centre of Basque nationhood and self-government. Since medieval times the Lords of Bizkaia had pledged to respect the liberties of the Basque people. The attack on Gernica was the first trial of the new tactic of saturation bombing being developed by Hitler's airforce, and was soon to be deployed with devastating effect across Europe. Gernica was completely destroyed in the course of three hours and many thousands were killed. But the Nationalists then tried to pretend that the attack was nothing to do with them, and that the town had been set on fire by 'the Reds' – the forces fighting for the Republic and against the Fascists. They even faked photos by placing large oil drums outside some of the larger buildings that had been destroyed. These can be seen in the museum in Gernica devoted to the atrocity and its aftermath.

[1] Gernica is the Basque spelling, Guernica the Spanish.

The lies of the Fascists did not go unchallenged, however. A British reporter for the London *Times*, George Steer, revealed the truth by visiting Gernica and citing evidence that proved conclusively that the town had been destroyed by bombing not by fire. His account in the *Times* and the *New York Times* made a profound impression on western opinion. A version of it in *L'Humanité* in Paris was read by Pablo Picasso, who was just beginning work on his commission from the Spanish Government for a large painting for the Spanish pavilion at the Paris ExPo that year. The painting he produced was *Guernica*, perhaps the most powerful piece of anti-war art ever created. The truth about Gernica did matter and did come out. The dictators were not able to suppress it, and the town became a symbol for the new horrors of modern warfare, because, as Steer showed, the town had no military significance. The munitions factory just outside was not bombed at all. The purpose of the attack was simply to intimidate and terrorize the civilian population and force them into submission.

Unhappily there have been many Gernicas since across the world. But the original story ends on a happier note. Although, aided by Hitler and Mussolini, the Fascists won the Spanish civil war, and the dictatorship Franco established lasted until his death in 1975, following the destruction of his allies in 1945, his regime lacked any moral legitimacy. After 1975 Spain returned to democracy, and gradually all the lies have been stripped away. The Fascist memorials to 'The Fallen' have been removed, and many of the institutions and practices which Franco sought to make permanent have been overturned. Spain has many internal problems, but it now has a functioning democracy and has taken its rightful place as one of Europe's leading states. The deep divide of the civil war and the scars which it left have slowly been erased. In the end Franco has not triumphed. He is like Ozymandias, and his lies have been buried along with him.

How Should Politics Be Studied?

One of the points of studying politics has always been to provide as objective and as comprehensive an account as possible of matters political. The study of politics has most often been called 'political science', particularly in the last hundred and fifty years. But what this political science involves, and the relationship of political scientists to *politics*, the subject matter of their discipline, have long been contested. There has always been a struggle between those who put the emphasis on 'science', wanting to make the discipline as methodologically rigorous and apolitical as possible, and those who put the emphasis on 'political', arguing what is the point of political science if it does not contribute to understanding the big political issues which confront us as citizens.

This has always been a central debate in the social sciences, ever since the *Methodenstreit*, the struggle or dispute over methods. This took place in the latter part of the nineteenth century, and pitched 'Austrian school' economists led by Carl Menger against historical economists led by Gustav Schmoller. The argument was over whether society and politics were best studied by building logical deductive models based on a few parsimonious assumptions about social reality, such as that all human beings seek to maximize their self-interest, or by historical, inductive arguments, trying to gather all the evidence that could be found to achieve as coherent a picture as possible of a particular period or problem.

This argument hardened into the divide between those who believed unwaveringly that there was an objective social reality which could be unlocked by the methods so successfully employed in the natural sciences, and those who thought that social reality was highly subjective and contested, and that the way to proceed was to interpret the meanings which different human beings gave to their actions. Society had to be studied from within not without.

A similar battle has raged within American political science since the founding of the American Political Science Association (APSA) at the end of the nineteenth century. The Association has grown to be much the largest national group of political scientists anywhere in the world. It has always had two main aims, which pull in different directions: to create as rigorous a science as possible, and to serve American democracy. This has become a debate about method, in particular whether political science should have one method or many methods, but it has also been a debate about relevance, whether political scientists should choose the subjects they study because of their importance as problems in real politics, or whether research agendas should be driven by the puzzles thrown up by increasingly technically sophisticated mathematical models and the research programmes of professional political scientists.

A widespread feeling amongst US political scientists in the early years of this century that the balance had swung too far towards the latter led to the 'perestroika' movement led by Theda Skocpol.

What is the Point of Studying Politics?

They argued that the discipline was in danger of losing its pluralism, and urged that much more attention both in teaching and research should be given to the big questions of contemporary politics – such as war, poverty, discrimination, global governance, and climate change.

The reformers had some success, but it was always qualified, and the argument keeps bursting out afresh. In a remarkable editorial published in 2015 in *Perspectives on Politics*, one of the key APSA journals, the editor, Jeffrey Isaac, raised a new flag of resistance.[2] The article argued for a more public political science. It attracted thousands of views on the journal website, rather more than the handful which most academic journal articles normally receive. The people who commented on the article before it was published included some of the most famous names in American political science: Peter Katzenstein, Ira Katznelson, Bob Keohane, Paul Pierson, and Kathy Thelen.

The article raised profound questions about what political science is today and what it means to be a political scientist, which affect all who study politics. These questions are not just about meth-

[2] Jeffrey Isaac, 'For a More *Public* Political Science', *Perspectives on Politics*, Vol. 13, June 2015, pp. 269–83.

74

odologies or approaches, but also about who can legitimately call themselves a political scientist in the future. Similar struggles have gone on in other disciplines, including economics and psychology, which have seen the progressive marginalization of approaches which were once well established, in some cases pushing them outside the discipline altogether.

It is hardly a secret that political science has always had a somewhat uneasy relationship with politics. That is because, as we saw in Chapter 1, many people consider politics rather disreputable, and this makes them suspicious of those who profess to study politics for a living. No good could come from studying politics. Those who did, like Hobbes and before him Machiavelli, were often thought to be masters of the dark arts. Introducing politics into universities might foment disorder. At Queen's College, Belfast, a professor was required to make a declaration promising, amongst other things, that he would not 'introduce or discuss any subject of politics or polemics, tending to produce contention or excitement'. When Queen's College became Queen's University in 1908, this stipulation was dropped, thus reducing the danger, as Howard Warrender noted in his inaugural lecture there in 1960, that 'a Professor of Political Science might lecture himself out of his Chair in the act of lecturing himself in'.

It was in the nineteenth century, when disciplinary boundaries were much more fluid than they are today, that this intellectual tradition of Political Science developed in Cambridge, associated in particular with the philosopher Henry Sidgwick and the historian John Seeley. By Political Science they did not mean the application of natural science methods to the study of politics. Rather it was a broad multidisciplinary inquiry, drawing on law, philosophy, history, and economics. They wanted to knit together all the different insights of thinking about the problems of government and provide an education suitable for those who would go out to rule the British Empire.

Seeley was the historian of the growth of the British Empire. He wrote a bestselling book called *The Expansion of England*, and wanted Political Science to be based on the empirical study of politics and history, collecting together a mass of facts and developing theory inductively from them. Sidgwick was the successor to John Stuart Mill as the main exponent of the utilitarian tradition, and wanted to equip his students with the ability to analyse the consequences of political action and choose the policies which could deliver the greatest happiness of the greatest number.

This idea of Political Science conceived it as Aristotle had done as the ultimate human science, integrating all other disciplines in the human sciences into a compelling whole, and providing a superior and useful education for the future governing elite. But the project did not survive. The pace of development in individual disciplines made it impractical for there to be one overarching discipline, and after Seeley and Sidgwick had departed, their empire was broken up and new faculties were established. In principle the Political Science they wanted would have had to incorporate all branches of study which have politically significant thought and action as their subject matter, and, given the accelerating growth of knowledge in the modern world, that would require lecturers and students with extraordinary abilities and encyclopaedic minds. It is an important corrective, however, to the contemporary tendency of learning more and more about less and less.

Politics has been taught under many labels, including political science, political studies, and just politics. In this book I use Politics with a capital 'P' to differentiate it from politics, the subject matter of the study of politics. It would be easier if all those who study politics were content to describe themselves as political scientists, but they are not, indeed some have always vehemently objected. In part this is just a simple confusion of language. Science in English has come to have a very firm association with the methods of the natural sciences. *Wissenschaft* in German, by contrast, simply refers to any organized and systematic body of knowledge, without laying down how the body of knowledge is organized or what methods should be employed.

What Keeps a Discipline Healthy?

Politics as an organized body of knowledge has retained something of the ideal of the original Cambridge idea of Political Science. Broad-based, interdisciplinary, eclectic approaches to the study of politics are still found in many countries throughout the world. The professionalization of the discipline is relatively recent, and much of the pressure for it has come from the United States. The subject has expanded rapidly in the last sixty years, with many new sub-fields and specialisms, and there has been a parallel development of international relations, and increasing integration between it and political science. Today Politics has become an established subject in every major international university. At the same time, there have been continuing controversies over where to set the limits to the study of politics, between, on the one hand, those who want to narrow it and further professionalize it by turning it into a discipline, establishing a core of agreed methods and theories, in order to prescribe what can and cannot be taught within it, and, on the other hand, those who have wanted to keep alive the broader, more eclectic vision of the older idea of Political Science. The idea of an academic discipline is always an unstable amalgam of forces. Disciplines are constantly being reshaped and reimagined, their cores disputed. Each new generation challenges some of the ideas held by the previous one, but there are certain principles which need to be observed if a discipline is to stay healthy and preserve the best parts of the tradition of study which it represents.

The first principle is openness – openness to other disciplines and other approaches. Politics should always resist turning in on itself, and treating its own methods and preoccupations as sacrosanct. Disciplinary boundaries exist but they are not fixed, and like national boundaries at the present time they are often irrelevant. Disciplines increasingly overlap. There are no tidy limits, and it is not desirable that there should be. Politics in the past has drawn on psychology, law, history, economics, sociology, and philosophy, among others. Politics, like the other human sciences, is a science of complex phenomena, and theoretical models designed to study simple phenomena and detect empirical regularities in order to make predictions are not sufficient on their own. Political reasoning can explain how or why something works the way it does, drawing on a toolkit of methods, but never relying on only one, because the aim is the most rounded understanding possible.

A second principle is that politics should focus on problems rather than on methodology. When a discipline like politics or international relations becomes concerned primarily with its own methods, and its practitioners with commenting upon each other's work rather than trying to find out something new about what is happening in the world, it starts to lose touch with what should be its main rationale. There are surely enough political problems in the world to keep us busy – whether it is conflict in Africa and the Middle East, the rise of India and China, the threat of climate change, the challenge of multiculturalism, the persistence of inequality and discrimination, rebuilding international prosperity, or tackling the migration crisis and restoring trust in the way democracy works.

Rudra Sil and Peter Katzenstein urge political scientists to draw on different theoretical constructs from competing research traditions to build complex arguments that bear on substantive problems of interest to both scholars and practitioners.[3] Such a research programme would seek engagement with the world of policy and practice; it would formulate problems wider in scope than the problems generated by mainstream research traditions in order to approximate the messiness and complexity of concrete dilemmas facing real-world actors; and it would offer complex causal stories, drawing on all the explanatory theories, models, and narratives embodied in competing research traditions.

A third principle is that Politics should aim for a balanced curriculum, built around some of its main approaches, which include political thought, political economy, comparative politics, and international relations. It needs to be able to help its students understand public policy in its broadest sense, through studying the contexts, the constraints, and the agencies that are at work in a variety of ways in politics across the globe. It needs to transcend the limits that have been put on the study of politics in

[3] Rudra Sil and Peter Katzenstein, *Beyond Paradigms: Analytical Eclecticism in the Study of World Politics* (London: Palgrave Macmillan, 2010).

the past by, for example, gendered or Eurocentric perspectives. Developing the ability to think critically about politics is not only valuable in itself but also a preparation for almost anything students of politics will go on to do.

A fourth principle is that one of the central purposes of an education in Politics is not just to develop the capacity to think critically but also to become acquainted with the nature of political reasoning. Every major discipline in the social sciences has developed its own form of reasoning to understand the complex phenomena it investigates. It is particularly evident in economics, but in an age when economic reasoning is tending to invade all aspects of social life, we should remember that other forms of reasoning are important too. Political reasoning is fundamentally concerned with understanding the limits to politics, what politics can achieve and what it cannot, and how best to deliver not only what we want but also what is necessary to sustain our common life.

A More Public Political Science

These are all themes which run through Jeffrey Isaac's manifesto 'For a More *Public* Political

What is the Point of Studying Politics?

Science', referred to above. His purpose, he says, is to clarify and expand the spaces where broad and problem-driven scholarly discussion and debates can flourish. The attempt to do this for the discipline of political science has parallels in the movements for public sociology and pluralist economics which have recently emerged in several countries. There have been successive waves of scientism and activism in Politics, and the discipline has at times fragmented into schools and sects. This fragmentation derives from commitments to both disciplinary and political pluralism which have been embedded in the study of politics from the beginning, but periodically there is a renewed search for intellectual unity and coherence. That often takes the form of trying to make the discipline more sophisticated as science, while those, like Isaac, who believe the focus should be on public relevance and public engagement argue that political scientists should be promoting broad public enlightenment and democratic civic engagement.

Isaac's view, however, is not the only one. The current challenge to a pluralist and publicly engaged Politics comes from those who argue that the social sciences are going through a major period of transition, with several disciplines moving from the humanities to the natural sciences in terms of research style, support needs, the availability of data, the empirical methods used, and the ability to make cumulative advances in understanding. Many social scientists no longer work primarily on their own but are increasingly involved in collaborative, interdisciplinary research teams.

One of the forms taken by this new pressure for intellectual unity in the discipline is a bid to unify quantitative and qualitative methods. This is to be achieved not only by new quantitative approaches to information collected by qualitative researchers, but also by data access and research transparency (DA-RT). The thinking behind DA-RT is that all empirical claims in Politics should be capable of being replicated, otherwise it is not a true science. In too many journal articles at the moment, it is claimed, this cannot be done. There is a lack of information on the selection of cases and in many cases data are not shared, either because they are withheld for some reason, or because they are just not made available. The aim of DA-RT is to rectify this by ensuring codification and enforcement of uniform standards of citation, data archiving, and presentation of evidence in order to achieve greater analytical and empirical rigour. Advocates of this approach point out that similar forms of scholarly modernization are taking place in other social scientific disciplines, notably psychology.

Isaac points out that what is distinctive about this new movement for intellectual unity is that rather than replacing qualitative methods with quantitative ones, it makes them conform to the same set of methodological criteria. Qualitative political science research is narrowly defined as the use of textual evidence to reconstruct causal mechanisms across a limited number of cases. Quantitative work uses an unlimited number. This implies that Politics at its core is a form of data analysis. For Isaac this raises fundamental questions of whether political science is a never-ending contest between different perspectives on politics or the understanding of the world as a set of objective processes. He compares the latter to what the philosopher John Dewey called 'the quest for certainty', a revival of the positivist belief that there is *a* truth which can be uncovered. Hypothesis testing becomes once more the gold standard of Politics research.

Isaac's view of the discipline is very different. He thinks the priority should not be more replicable research, but 'broader discussions and research projects which centre on ideas that are interesting and important'. There need to be spaces 'where scholars can develop creative and big ideas about how and why the political world works and how it might work differently'.[4] Which do we need more, he asks: a political science which is focused on the real political concerns facing the students we teach, or new and more rigorous data standards? The advocates of DA-RT suggest it should be the latter. A statement signed by the editors of many of the leading US political science journals (Isaac refused to sign on behalf of *Perspectives on Politics*) committed their journals to 'the principles of data access and research transparency, and implementing policies requiring authors to make as accessible as possible the empirical foundation and logic of inquiry of evidence-based research'.[5] The case is made not only on intellectual grounds, but also for the more practical reason that such a move makes it more likely that political science research will continue to receive support from funding agencies like the National Science Foundation.

Isaac's plea is that the search for intellectual rigour, important though that is to any scholarly enterprise, should not drown out the need to justify Politics by its relevance to the challenges of democratic citizenship. The study of politics is not like

---

[4] Isaac, 'For a More *Public* Political Science', pp. 276 and 277.
[5] *https://www.dartstatement.org/2014-journal-editors-statement-jets.*

the study of the natural world. The essential distinction between the human sciences and the natural sciences is once again in danger of being lost. For political scientists, as Isaac says, the key issue is how they should 'speak to but also *listen* to the complex and power-infused world that [they] both inhabit and take as [their] object of study'.[6] The advocates of DA-RT maintain that the main task should be to disseminate information of research findings which have been validated by the political science research community, rather than to find ways to be more open or engaged or interesting.

Journals become information containers or products, rather than spaces where ideas are represented, shared, contested, and then publicized. The DA-RT agenda is to maximize the replication of research findings, and one of the ways to do that is to purge research of all 'partiality', but that also risks purging it of relevance and significance. There is an important point here about what can and cannot be expected from political science research. Isaac is forthright: *Perspectives on Politics,* he argues, in common with every other political science journal, 'has published nothing that has settled once and for all any major analytical,

---

[6] Isaac, 'For a More *Public* Political Science', p. 277.

conceptual, empirical or normative dispute in political science'.[7]

The choice is stark: a broad-minded, ecumenical, intellectually serious, and politics-centred political science versus the accessibility and transparency of data and data analytical techniques. Isaac has no objection to quantitative political science and praises the insights it has brought. Politics is an organized body of knowledge, after all, which must always seek to be as objective as possible. But the question is: what kind of political science? Should it embrace a single method, or should it foster the development of a wide range of techniques, methods, experiments, arguments, and approaches?

How to Reason Politically

What is at stake is the preservation of particular forms of reasoning about the political world, which always used to be a large part of what the study of politics was about. If we take some representative figures from an earlier generation of scholars, such as Michael Oakeshott, John Maynard Keynes, Friedrich Hayek, and E.H. Carr, we can see that

---

[7] Isaac, 'For a More *Public* Political Science', p. 279.

they are all exemplars of particular modes of political reasoning – sceptical, rationalist, utopian, and realist – and often combined them to address what remains one of the great questions in politics: the scope and role of the state. None of them would have called himself a political scientist, but they all have something to teach us about what a problem-centred political science might look like.

Michael Oakeshott was Professor of Political Science at the London School of Economics in the 1950s. He was sceptical about the application of the methods of the natural sciences in the human sciences because they produced a rationalism which was deeply damaging to the traditions of a society, and in particular to the understandings which had formed about its political arrangements. Thinking about politics in rationalist and ideological terms meant for Oakeshott, as it had for Edmund Burke, mistaking the character of our politics and its limits, and led to ill-judged and inappropriate reforms. He favoured instead attending to the 'intimations' which were present in the traditions themselves.

Political activity, he wrote, is 'sailing on a boundless and bottomless sea. There is neither harbour for shelter nor floor for anchorage, neither starting place nor appointed destination. The enterprise is to keep afloat on an even keel; the sea is both friend and enemy.'[8] In order to cope with a situation which had no limits, politics needed to be very limited indeed in what it tried to attempt, and in its understanding of political action. For Oakeshott what was special about the European political tradition was the emergence of an understanding of the state as a civil association, a framework of general, non-instrumental law which left individuals free to make their own choices. It was threatened always by the rival understanding of the state as an enterprise association, which sought to harness all the energies of civil society in pursuit of a single goal, and in so doing made government unlimited, and potentially despotic.

John Maynard Keynes, by contrast, always belonged to the rationalist, confident, progressive side in politics. 'When the facts change, I change my mind. What do you do, sir?', he is once supposed to have said. He believed in the power of ideas and in the power of intellect. If the state was not an enterprise association, what was the good of the state? He thought it was perfectly possible to improve the world if people would only entrust their affairs to those like himself who had the capac-

---

[8] Michael Oakeshott, *Rationalism in Politics* (London: Methuen 1962), p. 127.

ity to make informed judgements. Keynes was not only a leading academic economist, but also a man of affairs who worked in the UK Treasury during both world wars. He thought that limits on government action should be set aside if there was a good reason for doing so. Keynes stands in a long tradition of English liberal reformers, going back to John Stuart Mill and Jeremy Bentham, who believed that the right institutions and policies can be designed which will promote greater happiness. Suffering and misery could be eroded; progress was feasible.

Keynes was convinced of the possibilities of enlightened reform and intelligent public policy. Faced by the realities of the slump in the 1930s, he devised practical policies for getting Britain out of it, arguing that the Government was imprisoned by dogmas which stopped it doing the things which should be done. Keynes helped lay the intellectual foundation for the great revolution in policy and the extension of the role of the state after 1945 which created the variegated structures of capitalism with which we are so familiar today, and which has still not been entirely reversed, despite everything that has happened in the last forty years. He argued that the 'important thing for Government is not to do things which individuals are doing already, and to do them a little better or a little worse, but to do those things which at present are not done at all'. He wrote to Friedrich Hayek in 1944 that 'Dangerous acts can be done safely in a community which thinks and feels rightly, which would be the way to hell if they were executed by those who think and feel wrongly.'[9]

Hayek was not reassured. In the 1930s he clashed with Keynes both theoretically and over matters of policy. Keynes once remarked that Hayek was an example of how a remorseless logician could start with a mistake and end up in bedlam. Not allowed to fight or to serve in government because of his Austrian connections, Hayek spent the war sitting in Cambridge writing *The Road to Serfdom*, his passionate denunciation of the drift to collectivism and the abandonment of the liberal principles of limited government on which, he argued, the success of modern western civilization had been based. Some of his views were close to those of Oakeshott, but Oakeshott always regarded Hayek as a utopian – a plan to resist all planning may be better than its opposite, he remarked, but it belongs to the same style of politics. To a greater extent than any of the other three, Hayek employed a utopian mode of

[9] J.M. Keynes, *Collected Writings*, Vol. XXVII (London: Macmillan 1980), pp. 387–8.

political reasoning. He became the most important inspiration behind the intellectual revival of liberal political economy, the champion of free markets and limited government, and warned constantly about the limits of human reason and human knowledge, and the consequent dangers of state involvement in the planning of the economy and civil society.

Although he was one of the fiercest critics of Keynes and still more of Keynesianism, which was developed by his followers after Keynes's death, they shared much in common. Both gave enormous importance to ideas, and both believed in the possibility of truth and progress. There was a right pattern to society which it was the duty of the state to recognize and to enable, using the coercive powers at its disposal. The state had to be limited in its functions but strong in carrying them out, to support the institutions of a free society. Hayek ultimately saw the state as an enterprise association in Oakeshott's sense. It had a supreme purpose: to encourage a political climate, a political movement, and political leaders able to reverse the extended state and re-establish a market order, in which political and administrative discretion would be reduced to the minimum, and individual liberty would flourish.

E.H. Carr studied classics before serving in the

Foreign Office for twenty years. He became the first holder of the chair in international relations at Aberystwyth, and wrote leaders for the London *Times*. In his later life he devoted himself to writing a history of Soviet Russia. Carr's sense of the political was substantially different from that of Keynes and Hayek because he put very little importance on the role of ideas in history and politics, and was scornful of idealist and utopian modes of political reasoning. On the contrary, he believed that history was shaped almost entirely by power and interests. One of his classic works, *The Twenty Years Crisis*, written on the eve of the Second World War, was a brutal exposure of the illusions entertained by liberal statesmen like Woodrow Wilson and liberal academics and commentators.

This did not make Carr a supporter of Churchill. In the 1930s he was a strong advocate of appeasement, based on his assessment of geopolitics and relative power relationships, and the options open to the democracies. He thought their position was hopeless. Carr belongs to a tradition of thinking about international relations which goes back to Thucydides in its emphasis on statecraft, and was to become a leading strand in international relations as an academic discipline after 1945. As he explained in *What is History?*, he did not believe it was the job of the historian to make moral judgements about personalities in history. He preferred to understand Stalin as the vehicle of vast impersonal forces, and argued that he owed his success to the dynamic force unleashed by the revolution.

Carr believed in progress but not in liberal progress. He thought that liberalism was finished, and that the world had outgrown it. The limits to politics for him were set by global economic and social forces, not ideas, and what happened in politics was a question not of human will, but of how well individuals understood the nature of their times and adapted to it. The constraints on human action were always more obvious to him than the opportunities for individuals to make a difference. He was accused by his critics of believing in determinism and inevitability and by Oakeshott of writing history as though it were retrospective politics, written from the standpoint of the victor. Carr was scornful of the pessimism among his contemporaries, their outdated faith that Europe was still the centre of the world, and their remoteness from real politics. During the war he pleaded to have some leave from his university post so that he could be more actively involved in the war. He never believed anything useful could be written on politics by anyone wholly isolated from current realities.

What is the Point of Studying Politics?

One of the points in studying politics is to test and improve our knowledge and to examine our beliefs. Socrates thought that the unexamined life was not worth living, and that is obviously true of our political lives. It is another reason for wanting to study politics. It allows us not just to study particular problems and political situations in depth, but also to spend time with the best minds, from many disciplines, who have reflected on the nature of politics and the political.

4

Can Politics Make a Better World?

The cultural critic Christopher Lasch asked in one of his last books, 'Why do serious people continue to believe in the future?'[1] The great promise of the modern world was that human beings would take control of their fate. This is what distinguished the modern world from all the stages of history which preceded it. The rational application of knowledge to industry and to society would mean rising prosperity and the gradual elimination of the evils of hunger, disease, and ignorance which had held back human progress for so long. Few of the philosophers of the European Enlightenment in the eighteenth century were starry-eyed optimists like Voltaire's satirical creation Dr Pangloss, who believed every-

[1] Christopher Lasch, *The True and Only Heaven: Progress and Its Critics* (New York: Norton, 1991), p. 530.

thing was for the best in the best of all possible worlds. Many remained pessimistic about human nature and fearful of democracy. But what united them was a belief in human reason and the benefits that could flow from its application to the many problems confronting human societies if only the right institutions could be put in place.

The Great Transformation

The Enlightenment philosophers lived and wrote only at the very beginning of the modern era. They could not have imagined the scale of the transformation that was about to happen. Looking back, we can now see that a remarkable new stage of human history began in the eighteenth and nineteenth centuries. Many of the conditions for it had been accumulating in many different societies and civilizations for several centuries, but the breakthrough when it came was still astounding. The table opposite tells the story.

After 1820, world gross domestic product (GDP) began to accelerate, growing by almost three times in the eighty years until 1900. In the first half of the twentieth century, despite two world wars, GDP more than doubled. In the next forty-two years it

Can Politics Make a Better World?

	World GDP $ Trillion	World Population Billion
1820	0.7	1
1900	2	1.6
1950	5	2.5
1992	28	5.3
2018	78	7.6

increased more than five times, and in the two decades since 1992, following the end of the cold war and the entry of China and India into the international economy, it has almost tripled. In the last two hundred years world GDP has shown cumulative growth – a break with previous human experience of at best cyclical growth. At the same time, world population took off. It has now increased by just over seven times since 1820, with the fastest increase coming since 1950. Similarly, energy use from a very low level in 1820 rose forty times up to 2000, from 250 million metric tons of oil equivalent in 1820 to 800 million metric tons in 1900 and to 10,000 million metric tons in 2000.

Before the modern era, output and population grew very slowly, if at all, and often went backwards. The experience from the late eighteenth century onwards was unprecedented. Human societies were used to cyclical growth. What was new was cumulative growth so that the starting point for each new cycle was higher than the last. After several generations of economic growth and population growth, the expectation that this was now normal became ingrained.

The modern world was dominated at first by the European great powers, then later by the United States, which after 1945 worked to form a united West under its leadership. The Europeans used their new resources and superior technology to colonize large areas of the world, extracting huge resources as they did so. For a time it seemed to assure their permanent dominance. The countries which were the leading powers and leading economies in 1900 were the same in 2000, with the exception of Japan. But no-one expects the list will be the same in 2050, still less in 2100. The process of capitalist globalization at the end of the twentieth century created the conditions for a major shift in world politics as India and China began to modernize their economies and participate in international trade. Huge numbers were lifted out of poverty as a result of China's rise, and the Eurocentric character of modernity was shattered.

Globalization is not a single uniform process. There are many globalizations, and not just the western version. All countries in the world have crossed the threshold into modernity, which has implications for their economies, their cultures, and their politics. In 2000 the UN noted that for the first time a majority of the world's population was living in cities rather than on the land. The eight Millennium Development Goals set by the UN had been substantially achieved by the target date of 2015. Great inequality and great unevenness remain, both between countries and within countries, but the world has been transformed and there is no going back. Change is continuing to happen, and at an accelerating rate.

The Debate on Progress

Many of the hopes of nineteenth-century believers in progress, however, have not been realized. They expected that as nations grew more prosperous, they would trade more with one another and become more peaceful. The twentieth century was a rude setback to those hopes. There were world wars, genocides, and famines. After 1918, and again after 1945 and 1991 with the ending of the cold war, there were hopes for a universal peace. That has not happened. But despite all the reverses there has been real progress as well. Many evils that once existed, such as slavery, have been overcome or greatly reduced, and many diseases eradicated or contained. There has been a marked reduction in violence between societies and within societies. Numbers in absolute poverty have diminished, particularly in the last thirty years.

This has not been enough to convince the sceptics. Even as some older problems have diminished, new problems have crowded in. The human species is in a race against itself. The speed with which it has gained new knowledge and wealth in the last two hundred years has unleashed an accelerating wave of technology which has brought with it new perils which are hard to estimate precisely, but which shadow our future. The proliferation of nuclear weapons and the effect of human activity on the environment and the climate are the greatest of these, but there are several others, such as the rise of artificial intelligence with its potential effect in destroying employment, and new medical technologies which may transform the natural human life cycle.

Many technological changes bring great advantages, but there is concern whether human societies can adjust fast enough, and in particular how politics can manage the transition and the conflicts of interest and profound issues of principle likely to arise. Alongside these are more long-standing challenges such as poverty and inequality, as well as the threats to economic prosperity in the shape of debt and stagnation, and the threats to international governance in the shape of populist nationalism and the difficulties of extending institutions of multilateral cooperation.

The scale of the challenges is in marked contrast to the relative paucity of the means to deal with them. This is why many people wonder if instead of gaining control over our fate we are steadily losing it. Is progress going into reverse? Is the very knowledge that made it possible to think of making the world a better place in danger of destroying us? The physicist Martin Rees called his book on the challenges the human race faces from the unintended consequences of its own technologies, *Our Final Century*.[2] He analyses the different threats facing us, from terrorism and nuclear proliferation to climate change and genetic modification and artificial intelligence.

But there are also optimists, like the psychologist Steven Pinker, who has written a resounding defence of the Enlightenment tradition, arguing that despite the mood of profound cultural

[2] Martin Rees, *Our Final Century* (London: Heinemann, 2003).

103

pessimism in the western democracies, the evidence shows overwhelmingly that human societies in the last two hundred years have become less violent, more prosperous, more peaceful, and more socially liberal than ever before.[3] He accepts that there are still big problems to address, but argues that we will not be able to tackle them if we turn our backs on the very ideas and institutions which have brought us to our current stage. If human societies stick with science and take the advice of experts, human behaviour can adjust to allow many of the challenges to be tackled. But what is also needed is a creative politics which can build new multilateral institutions and agreements. It can be done. In 1976 scientists found that the ozone layer in the earth's atmosphere which absorbs the ultra-violet radiation of the sun was being seriously depleted by the uncontrolled release of certain chemical compounds, CFCs, across the world. An international treaty to ban CFCs was finally agreed in 1986, and all 197 members of the UN have now signed it. The ozone layer has substantially recovered since the signing of the treaty. It shows that politics can work.

[3] Steven Pinker, *Enlightenment Now: The Case for Reason, Science, Humanism, and Progress* (London: Penguin, 2017).

We need similar agreements to deal with species extinction and many other threats.

Radical or Sceptic?

If this is the world we inhabit, how should we react? Should you be a radical or a sceptic about politics? Should you be engaged or disengaged? Many people become interested in politics and want to study it because they are passionately attached to a particular cause, or because they are stirred by a particular event or injustice. You feel that something is wrong and you want to change it. Wanting to make the world a better place has always been a spur to action. If something is manifestly wrong, you want to know how it can be put right, and more than that, you want to know how it arose in the first place.

Being committed should not stop you respecting established norms of discourse and canons of evidence in developing your arguments. It will make them more effective. Such rules distinguish any disciplined form of inquiry from polemic, speculation, and personal opinion, and it is vital we hold on to them even when we strongly disagree with one another. To work well, politics requires a degree of civility, tolerance, and mutual respect. What is required of every citizen is to be prepared to question the evidence for their own beliefs and commitments, and to be prepared to admit error. Oliver Cromwell once urged intransigent Scottish opponents of his policies: 'I beseech you, in the bowels of Christ, think it possible that you may be mistaken.' It is a maxim we should all follow.

If disagreements are not to turn violent, we have to find ways of agreeing to disagree, and coming to decisions which do not involve us fighting one another. This can be hard when both sides to a divide believe that not only the facts but also the right is on their side. The most dangerous moment in democracies comes when one side is not persuaded that a decision that has been taken is legitimate, or that it is an issue of such importance to them that they cannot accept the result. Such watershed events, like the American civil war or the Irish civil war, can divide societies for generations. Even events which do not lead to civil war, like the Brexit Referendum in the UK, can have a comparable effect, creating new political alignments by dividing old from young, the large cities from the small towns, the more educated from the less educated, cosmopolitans from nativists.

Some distrust the passions which politics can

arouse; the dividing of everyone into friends and enemies; the disregard for rational argument and evidence; the abandonment of compromise. This leads many to disengage altogether. Others choose to take a contemplative rather than an engaged stance towards politics. They deliberately set themselves apart from the intense commitments and struggles of everyday politics, the better to understand the more fundamental determinants of the events and outcomes of the political world. A sceptical and critical position in politics can seem the best vantage point from which to assess the rival certainties which compete for our attention. Sometimes it seems that there is no solid ground anywhere because of the collapse of faith in the future, both religious and secular.

Must we choose between scepticism and radicalism, or between realism and utopianism? Any mature form of political understanding needs to draw on many different modes of reasoning if it is to grasp the nature of conflict in human societies, and its roots in our capacity to develop different interests, to hold different values, to form different identities, and to come to different judgements. Studying almost any political problem forces us to acknowledge the complexity and intractability of political situations, their dark side as well as their absurd side. Risk, uncertainty, and contingency are unavoidable features of the political world. We are confronted by a plethora of competing and incompatible claims, so it is not surprising that scepticism about our ability to choose between them, still less to reconcile them, is rife.

What also gives force to sceptical analyses of the limits of politics is the scale of so many of the problems when coupled with the inadequacies of human reason, human capacities, human knowledge, and the frailties of human will. Politics, other than in the most minimal terms, can often seem a futile exercise. There is a continual contrast between political rhetoric and political accomplishment, and the sceptic will argue that this must always be so, and that its reasons lie deep within the nature of politics and human beings; the folly and presumption of human ambition, which suggest the need for humility in the face of the problems that human societies face; and a preference for the prudential, the tried, and the known.

To think seriously about politics we need scepticism. Karl Marx's motto was 'doubt everything'. But politics cannot just be about scepticism. We also need Kant's injunction: *sapere aude*, dare to know. Politics is also about imagination, possibility, and hope. To be effective in politics you have to

Can Politics Make a Better World?

understand the constraints within which you must operate. But every so often someone challenges the constraints, and overturns what was up to then considered politically impossible or politically unthinkable. Martin Luther King did this. Nelson Mandela did this. So did Margaret Thatcher. Politics would have much less claim on our attention if, as well as being steeped in a clear-eyed realism about the circumstances of the world, it was not also by turns a theatre of dreams and limitless possibility. No-one captured this better than Nietzsche, who declared in his last book, *Ecce Homo*:

> I know my fate. One day my name will be associated with the memory of something tremendous – a crisis without equal on earth, the most profound collision of conscience, a decision that was conjured up *against* everything that had been believed, demanded, hallowed so far. I am no man, I am dynamite. ... It is only beginning with me that the earth knows *great politics*.[4]

New political movements bubbling up from the bottom to challenge established patterns of power and privilege have always been inspired by the potential to create a better world. Tom Paine,

---

[4] Friedrich Nietzsche, *On the Genealogy of Morals/Homo*, trans. Walter Kaufman (New York: Vintage, 1989), pp. 326–7.

109

the eighteenth-century radical and author of *Commonsense* and *The Rights of Man*, wrote that having a hand in two revolutions (the American and the French) was living to some purpose. The modern era in particular has seen periodic surges of hope, which have fuelled sometimes millenarian beliefs in a brighter and better future, and contributed to the idealism of revolutions. Many of these revolutions, like the recent Arab Spring, which swept many countries in the Middle East, have ended in failure and disillusion, but often they have left positive legacies as well. Despite the failures and despite the disillusion, the irrepressible optimism of human beings aided by the rise of new generations constantly inspires new beginnings.

The sceptical counterpoint to the utopians and the revolutionaries is that the most that politics can do is to seek 'shelter in our time', to try to prevent really bad things happening, to seek to improve societies inch by inch, by correcting mistakes, a process of trial and error. Both have their place. Politics needs enthusiasm and commitment; it also needs pragmatism and realism. There is an endless cycle at work between these two. If there was no passionate intensity in politics, the modern world itself would not have come about, as even an arch-sceptic like Michael Oakeshott recognized

Can Politics Make a Better World?

in his essay *The Politics of Faith and the Politics of Scepticism.*[5] Realists acknowledge the unavoidable constraints on human action which arise from the way in which the world is structured and power is distributed. If politicians want to be effective in what they do, they must first understand the nature of these constraints.

They cannot succeed by ignoring them, or pretending that they do not exist, and if they do, they risk achieving something quite different from what they intended. Realism as a form of political reasoning emphasizes realities and therefore tends towards determinism and fatalism, but there are also strands of realism which see the acknowledgement of realities and constraints as the basis for radical transformation. For realists, politics has less to do with ideas and values than with configurations of power. Some think that the constraints on political action are endlessly the same, and there is no way to break out of them, but others argue that the development of the modern world constantly creates new structures and new opportunities, which the successful politician can seize. Yet the opportunities come from the structures, so politicians must work

[5] Michael Oakeshott, *The Politics of Faith and the Politics of Scepticism*, ed. Timothy Fuller (New Haven: Yale University Press, 1996).

within these structures; they cannot ignore them or abolish them if they want to succeed.

Rationalists and idealists go further. They seek moral change, or institutional change, and sometimes both at once. They are much more likely to emphasize the opportunities for politicians and political movements to make a difference, to alleviate suffering, to reduce inequality, and to achieve the dream of a more just and equal society, not just where they live but throughout the world. Bertrand Russell was a supreme rationalist and a radical. In contrast to those who as they age become more sceptical and disillusioned about politics, Russell grew more engaged. A life-long campaigner against war and imperialism, in his eighties he became one of the leaders of the Campaign for Nuclear Disarmament during the 1950s and was arrested and briefly imprisoned. He wrote a short book in 1919 called *Political Ideals*. Almost half a century later it was one of the first books on politics, together with Carr's *What is History?*, that I ever possessed. It still captures for me the excitement of discovering politics, and the realization of what a rich store of writing on politics and the political existed, on its limitations and on its possibilities. Russell in this book spoke to its possibilities (in the gendered language of the time):

Can Politics Make a Better World?

> Few men seem to realise how many of the evils from which we suffer are wholly unnecessary, and they could be abolished by a united effort within a few years. If a majority in every civilised country so desired, we could, within twenty years, abolish all abject poverty, quite half the illness in the world, the whole economic slavery which binds down nine tenths of our population; we could fill the world with beauty and joy, and secure the reign of universal peace. It is only because men are apathetic that this is not achieved, only because imagination is sluggish, and what always has been is regarded as what always must be. With goodwill, generosity, intelligence, these things could be brought about.[6]

Sceptics and realists alike snort with derision at such sentiments. In the eighteenth century Joseph de Maistre mocked Rousseau's claim that human beings were born free but were everywhere in chains. It was, he said, like declaring that sheep were born carnivorous, but everywhere nibble grass. Russell wrote the lines quoted above one hundred years ago, at the end of a world war which, as we noted in Chapter 1, had claimed 20 million dead and during which he had been imprisoned as a conscientious objector. Twenty years later the world plunged into

---

[6] Bertrand Russell, *Political Ideals* (London: Allen & Unwin, 1963), p. 25.

113

the Second World War, an even greater cataclysm, which left 70 million dead. Political idealism is generally less in fashion than it was, although the political world can still be swept by sudden gusts of hope, often focused on particular leaders, such as Nelson Mandela or Aung San Suu Kyi, who both become powerful symbols of resistance to injustice and of the struggle for freedom. Nelson Mandela is still revered, but Aung San Suu Kyi's reputation has lost its lustre because of her failure to speak out on the plight of the Rohingya people driven from their homes by the military in Myanmar.

Why Politics Matters

Sceptical and realist assessments of the limits of politics are an essential part of the craft of politics. But they also themselves have their limits, since if taken too far they fuel the kind of apathy and disengagement from politics with which we are too familiar. On any historical assessment the achievement of some form of limited democracy in so many countries today is an extraordinary one, even if much more fragile and less certain than we would wish. Many sceptics and realists today think it is transient, but their reasons are often different. Sceptics think that democracy can never work, while realists point to the structures which prevent the ideals of democracy from ever being achieved in practice. All this is part of the mood of disaffection with politics of all kinds, and the spread of cynicism and detachment, expressed in falling participation in elections, and the collapse of trust in politics and politicians – the mood that 'Nothing Works'. Such a mood, fanned by parts of the media, narrows the limits of politics, because it is corrosive of the idea of a public realm, and of citizenship. Politics comes to be regarded as a corrupt and self-seeking activity. If such attitudes become widespread, then the capacity of politics to affect change also shrinks.

Reform agendas which draw on idealist and rationalist modes of political reasoning often face an uphill struggle, but they remain an essential ingredient of our politics. This is partly because, despite all the cynicism, citizens still periodically can be lured into putting their trust in a new charismatic political leader, like Barack Obama or Emmanuel Macron. There is a periodic suspension of disbelief before the inevitable disillusionment. Enoch Powell, the maverick English Tory, wrote that 'all political careers end in failure, because that is the nature of human affairs'. But some political careers fail less obviously than others. Powell's seemed to have decisively failed at the time of his death in 1998. All the causes he had campaigned so hard for seemed lost. Yet less than twenty years later, one of the causes he had made his own and defined for a generation of Eurosceptics, opposition to Britain being part of the European Union, received a belated and triumphant endorsement in the 2016 Referendum. The hope that some substantial change for the better might finally be delivered through politics remains enormously powerful in all modern cultures, since human beings remain on balance, and probably against the weight of evidence, remarkably optimistic. They have the future in their bones, as Carr said; unlike intellectuals, he added sourly.[7]

It is also because of the huge change which modernity has wrought on our world. Spontaneously, collectively, and without anyone planning it, the human race in the last two hundred years has embarked on a gigantic uncontrolled experiment which is steadily transforming the conditions of life for everyone on the planet. As John McNeill has written, we have begun to play dice with the planet without knowing all the rules of the game.[8]

[7] Jonathan Haslam, *The Vices of Integrity: E.H.Carr 1892–1982* (London: Verso, 1999), p. 180.
[8] John McNeill, *Something New Under the Sun: An Environmental History of the Twentieth Century* (London: Penguin, 2001).

This is not a situation from which any individual or any society can opt out. The consequences are all around us and are multiplying. The challenges which human societies now face are of a different order of magnitude to the past, and our capacities for meeting them are seriously inadequate.

A sceptical response is understandable, but if pushed too far it becomes an abdication of responsibility. Simply shrugging our shoulders and concentrating on looking after our own immediate interests is beguiling, but also a betrayal. A realist response directs us to the enormity of the transformation which is taking place, and the scale of the problems confronting us. But a realist response by itself is not enough, since there is no reason to think that the problems will be sorted by themselves. A reform agenda is also needed, which can knit together the different elements to provide the kind of new institutions and rules, the new governance arrangements that are necessary if the human race is to have any future at all, and can also bring about a moral change. The limits of politics are clear enough from past experience, but they have also to be overcome if appropriate remedies for the problems we face are to be adopted in time. There can be no more urgent task confronting us today than to use all our energy and our understanding to ensure that they are.

Politics does matter, and we should be bothered about it. There is too much at stake for us not to be. That is why we need to learn more about it, to become better and more engaged citizens. Politics is always going to be messy, often distasteful, sometimes profoundly depressing, but at other times it can be exhilarating, liberating, and absorbing. It is never dull. That is why people have always been drawn to study politics. It is an inescapable part of our human experience. We can deny it and try to shut it out. But we have no choice. We can hardly avoid participating in politics and learning about politics. Even non-participation is a political act.

Sometimes those who denigrate politics sound like John Cleese in Monty Python's film *The Life of Brian* rhetorically demanding, 'What have the Romans ever done for us?' Even after his followers' suggestions – aqueducts, sanitation, roads, medicine, education, health, wine, public baths, public order, and peace – he still repeats the question. Apart from all those things, what have the Romans done for us? We might similarly ask: what has politics done for us? One of the most eloquent recent answers to this comes from the

Can Politics Make a Better World?

German President, Frank-Walter Steinmeier. In a speech on 19 June 2018 opening the Thomas Mann House in Los Angeles he spoke about democracy and the current threats to it around the world. Thomas Mann when young had been a nationalist and an anti-democrat, but the aftermath of the First World War and the fragile democracy of the Weimar Republic changed his views. It had become much easier to criticize than to defend it. Mann decided to take a stand, breaking with many of his former political associates and earning Hitler's undying enmity. But as Mann said, 'It is a terrible spectacle when irrationalism becomes popular.' His response, as Steinmeier says, has extraordinary relevance today. Mann wrote: 'Refusal on the part of the intellect to engage with politics is an error and a self-deception. One does not get clear of politics in that way. One only ends up on the wrong side. A-political simply means anti-democratic.' Steinmeier pleads that in the face of the rise of populist nationalism in the United States and in Europe and in many other parts of the world, the response to irrationalism must not be a retreat from politics, and certainly not contempt for politics. As he puts it, 'In the light of current events, I want to say that it is now up to us to make sure it does not become easier once again to defame democracy than to defend it.'[9]

The building of a peaceful, prosperous, and democratic Europe after 1945 was one of the great political achievements of the twentieth century. Many individual politicians contributed to that outcome on both sides of the Atlantic through the treaties which established NATO and the European Economic Community (which evolved into the European Union). In a fit of amnesia or worse, significant elements in the United States and Europe now want to tear down the multilateral rules-based order which has delivered so much in the last seventy years, and go back to the fragmented and much more dangerous world of aggressive nationalisms. Steinmeier eloquently reminds us of what is at stake and what we could lose, and who the enemies of democracy are. This is why politics matters.

[9] *http://www.bundespraesident.de/SharedDocs/Downloads/DE/Red en/2018/06/180619-USA-Konferenz-Demokratie-Englisch-2.pdf?__ blob=publicationFile.*

Further Reading

There is a lot of great and engaging writing about politics. The best way to start is just to dive in and sample a wide range of views and approaches. Always question what you read, including this book, and seek out alternative opinions and perspectives, asking what is the evidence on which their claims are based. That way you can learn to form your own independent judgements and develop your capacity for critical thinking. Becoming politically aware means wanting to engage in politics and to study politics. There is a vast ocean of contradictory facts, opinions, and beliefs. Here are a few pointers to get started.

A modern classic on politics is Bernard Crick, *In Defence of Politics* (fifth edition; London: Continuum, 2000). First published in 1962, it stands out for its passionate defence of democratic politics as the only alternative human beings have discovered to coercion and despotism. More recent general books on politics which have something important to say include Gerry Stoker, *Why Politics Matters* (second edition; London: Palgrave Macmillan, 2017), Colin Hay, *Why We Hate Politics* (Cambridge: Polity, 2007), Matt Flinders, *Defending Politics: Why Democracy Matters in the Twenty-First Century* (Oxford: Oxford University Press, 2012), and David Runciman, *Politics* (London: Profile Books, 2014). For a conservative libertarian take on politics, try Kenneth Minogue, *Politics: A Very Short Introduction* (Oxford: Oxford University Press, 1995).

One of the best books on democracy is John Dunn, *Setting the People Free: The Story of Democracy* (Princeton, NJ: Princeton University Press, 2018). It is a good introduction to his many other books on politics, and to his distinctive sceptical voice. If you want an antidote to scepticism, try Hilary Wainwright, *A New Politics from the Left* (Cambridge: Polity, 2018), which overflows with passionate engagement and hope for the future. Mary Beard, *Women and Power: A Manifesto* (London: Profile Books, 2017), also offers a rousing call for action and a strong account of why the revolution in gender relationships started by the suffragettes is still far from complete.

The case against progress, and continuing to believe that it is possible in human affairs, is powerfully made by John Gray in a collection of his essays, *Gray's Anatomy: Selected Writings* (London: Penguin, 2013). The opposite view is trenchantly put by Steven Pinker, *Enlightenment Now: The Case for Reason, Science, Humanism and Progress* (London: Penguin, 2018). This is one of the great political debates of our time. Have a look also at Martin Rees, *Our Final Century* (London: Heinemann, 2003), and John McNeill, *Something New Under the Sun: An Environmental History of the Twentieth Century* (London: Penguin, 2001). Naomi Klein has also written with great power on the politics of climate change: *This Changes Everything: Capitalism Against the Climate* (New York: Simon & Schuster, 2014). For a sceptical view on the science of climate change (by a non-scientist), see Nigel Lawson, *An Appeal to Reason: A Cool Look at Global Warming* (London: Duckworth, 2009), and for an optimistic take on how human societies can adjust to climate change, try Matt Ridley, *The Rational Optimist* (London: Fourth Estate, 2011).

A starting point for thinking about international relations is Thucydides, *History of the*

Peloponnesian War. (Many translations are available. My personal favourite is by Jeremy Mynott, *The War of the Peloponnesians and the Athenians* [Cambridge: Cambridge University Press, 2013].) An excellent guide to it can be found in Geoffrey Hawthorn, *Thucydides on Politics* (Cambridge: Cambridge University Press, 2014). On contemporary international relations a very good overview is James Mayall, *World Politics: Progress and Its Limits* (Cambridge: Polity, 2000). See also Paul Hirst, *War and Power in the Twenty-First Century* (Cambridge: Polity, 2000), and the sober analysis by Furio Cerutti, *Global Challenges for Leviathan: A Political Philosophy of Nuclear Weapons and Global Warming* (Lanham, MD: Lexington Books, 2007).

A foundation for thinking about politics is a knowledge of the classics of political thought. *Cambridge Texts in the History of Political Thought* is a magnificent series which provides annotated texts of classic works in the western tradition of political thought with critical introductions. Steven Lukes has written an engaging introduction to some of the great controversies in western political thought in the form of a picaresque novel, *The Curious Enlightenment of Professor Caritat: A Novel of Ideas* (London: Verso, 2009). See also

Further Reading

Alan Ryan's absorbing study of political ideas, *On Politics* (London: Allen Lane, 2012). One of the problems with the western tradition of political thought is that it is western and that until recently it was largely written by men about men. Carole Pateman in *The Sexual Contract* (Cambridge: Polity, 1988), exposes the assumptions about gender which underpin it.

It is always useful to have some reference books to hand to be reminded of the many contested meanings of the ideas and concepts used in politics. Roger Scruton, *A Dictionary of Political Thought* (London: Palgrave Macmillan, 2007), is an admirably succinct and lucid guide, flavoured with the author's strong political views. Raymond Williams, *Keywords* (London: Fourth Estate, 1988), is endlessly illuminating about how our political language evolved.

There are also many novels, poems, films, art, and blogs to explore. Studying politics is not just about turgid academic volumes. Films like *Dr Strangelove*, *The Great Dictator*, *Z*, *Blade Runner*, *Cry Freedom*, *Gandhi*, *The Battle of Algiers*, *All the President's Men*, *Frost–Nixon*, *Citizen Kane* (very topical just now), and many others greatly enrich the study of politics, as does great art like Picasso's *Guernica* and Lorenzetti's *Allegory of Good Government*. It is the same with the blogosphere. The resources of the world wide web have brought an amazing array of resources within easy reach. There never was such a good time to be studying politics.